WIN THAT JOB

WIN THAT JOB

E. L. Mayoh

foulsham
LONDON · NEW YORK · TORONTO · SYDNEY

foulsham
Yeovil Road, Slough, Berkshire SL1 4JH

ISBN 0–572–01490–2

Printed in Great Britain at St. Edmundsbury Press,
Bury St. Edmunds.

CONTENTS

1 INTRODUCTION

How important is it for you to have a good job?

How worthwhile is it to have satisfying work in the company of colleagues who value your opinion; where you look forward to the day-to-day challenges and take pride in your achievements; where your efforts are rewarded by a good income and prospects for further advancement and you have plenty of opportunity to use your skills and develop your knowledge and experience?

The choice of occupation is one of the most important that most of us will ever make. It influences how we feel and affects all aspects of family life — where we live, our standard of living and social activities, even our circle of friends and acquaintances. Winning the job of your choice will give you a sense of fulfilment and can change your whole outlook on life and on your future prospects. Any decision, preparation and application for a job deserves all the time and trouble you can muster!

In practice, most people spend more time in preparing their car for re-sale or in decorating and improving their house when they are hoping for a good price than they would dream of spending in developing any skill in applying for a new job. Many hopefuls apply for jobs in a haphazard manner — their applications are unimpressive and, if they do receive an invitation to attend for interview they are so ill prepared that they give a very poor account of themselves.

Of course, each individual's situation is unique to him or her. Some readers will never have experienced normal employment (a number of you will still be receiving full-time education and may be unsure about the formalities of job-seeking), others may have been made redundant or will be looking for a post with better prospects, even seeking senior executive posts; some will have had trouble convincing employers that they have enough to offer because they are too young or inexperienced, or have been made to feel that they are too old, and that their experience and qualifications are inappropriate.

When a vacancy is on offer it is not necessarily the best candidate who is offered the job: the successful person is the one who convinces the employer that he or she is better than anyone else available. This book offers everyone who is seeking new employment the opportunity to make such an impact on prospective employers that the possibility of being appointed to the post on offer will be increased enormously.

Make no mistake, however, there is no magic solution on offer. It will still be the applicant who must convince the employer that he or she is the right person for the job — this book is not a substitute for effort on the part of the candidate. What it *will* do is to help anyone who puts into practice the recommended methods and techniques to present an application which will so impress the employer that an invitation for interview will probably follow. Having negotiated that difficult hurdle, the interview situation can then be approached with confidence, especially after the preparation which candidates are helped to make in the following pages.

Job hunting is a skill in itself. It is not enough to be good at your work; you must be able to convince an employer that you would do well in the job on offer.

It can be stated with confidence and conviction that every person who is seriously seeking a job will discover, after following the advice and suggestions which follow, that applications and interview performance will show a remarkable improvement — and your self-confidence will be increased enormously.

2 SETTING THE SCENE

There are many people who send away one application after another for jobs which they believe they have some chance of getting, but find that they are seldom offered an interview — on the rare occasions when an employer asks to meet them nothing comes of it, and after the interview they feel that they have let themselves down, once again.

Why is it that most job applications fail?

This persistent poor performance is the result of many factors, but mainly it will be found that too little thought was given to style, presentation and content of the written application; there was not enough consideration taken of what the employer was seeking and of how to convince him that the writer had the qualities to meet those needs.

The most common reason for consistent failure in the interview situation is the lack of adequate preparation by the candidate — a meeting which allows the opportunity to satisfy an interviewer that he is the right person for the job can often become a humiliating experience with the applicant feeling more and more nervous, ill at ease and tongue-tied (or too talkative), eventually leaving convinced that he failed to do himself justice.

Guide your own destiny

There are a number of myths associated with success. It is a commonly held belief that only brilliant individuals get to the top of their profession, or make their mark in industry. A close study of a number of such people will quickly reveal, however, that a record of brilliance is the exception rather than the rule; most people in top jobs have got to where they are through sheer determination and hard work, usually accompanied by a sense of purpose.

You may say that some people are lucky; that you know of people who have got on because of some extraordinary stroke of luck or because they knew the "right" people. Although exceptionally this may be true, generally speaking we all make our own luck and it is hard work and perseverance which pay off in the long run. You may have heard the story of the famous golfer playing in a national tournament whose shot bounced off a hillock at the side of the green to within inches of the hole. A spectator shouted "How lucky can you get?" The golfer looked around and replied, "Yes. The more I practise the luckier I am!" There is no substitute for persistence and the will to succeed.

After a number of rejections it is all too easy to feel frustrated, and many people lose heart at this stage, making only feeble attempts to secure the job they really want. It is essential to keep plugging away — what you will read in the following pages will encourage you to believe that with a little organisation, some self-analysis, good presentation of written applications and adequate preparation for interviews you will eventually achieve your goal.

Keep your standards high

As most applicants prepare their job applications and prime themselves for their interviews in their own homes, it is easy to forget that this is an area of endeavour where there can be fierce competition, particularly in recent years when jobs have become more difficult to get. But there are still many thousands of vacancies waiting to be filled every week and the people who are successful in being appointed to these jobs are usually those who have taken a little more trouble than their competitors. Okay, it may take a little longer than it would have done when competition wasn't so fierce, but if you persevere and keep your standards high you should succeed. Even failure can have its positive side since quite a lot can be learned from your mistakes if you have the courage and self-discipline to examine your performance in retrospect.

Win That Job provides guidance in the following areas: assessing your own experience and abilities and evaluating these against the jobs available; completing written applications in a manner which is likely to make a favourable impression on the employer; anticipating the questions which are likely to be asked in the interview; preparing for that interview; and above all, acquiring and building confidence in yourself and in your ability to show would-be employers that you are the person they should employ.

3 BASIC PREPARATION

The principles and methods outlined in the following pages will, if followed with determination, vastly improve the likelihood of your being offered the job of your choice.

Every person's qualifications, experience, personal circumstances, motives, objectives and aspirations are unique to that individual, yet there will be very few people indeed who will not substantially enhance their job prospects by reading and putting into practice what is set out in this book. The advice and procedures you will find here will benefit most job-seekers whether teenage school leavers or redundancy victims of 60, those whose ambition is for nothing more than a secure, pleasant job with an average income, or senior executives seeking more rewarding posts.

Organisation and record-keeping

If you are to realise the maximum benefit from what you read here then you must impose upon yourself a measure of self-discipline. You need to have a methodical approach to your quest for a job and it is not too difficult to adopt a simple routine and allocate some time on specified days of each week to up-dating your records, checking deadlines, seeking vacancies, acquiring information, writing applications and follow-up letters, etc.

I am not suggesting that you become obsessional in your approach — rather that you determine to turn your back on the haphazard and unproductive methods which many of your competitors use.

Personal History file

As a basis for your endeavours the first and one of the most important tasks is to make a comprehensive list of all relevant data about yourself, your background, experience and interests. This list might take a little time to compile since you will want to make it as full as possible. Don't forget to list those qualities or experiences which you might take for granted and possibly seem uncon-

11

nected to job applications; these very "irrelevancies" may just tip the scales for one particular job or with an employer who is looking beyond the obvious.

You will need to refer to this Personal History record each time you make a formal written application and will need to keep it close at hand even when making informal enquiries, as mentioned later. When an application appears to require, in your judgement, additional information then you will add this information to the master copy of your Personal History. In time a very complete picture of your background will have been built up. Needless to say, you would not always choose to use all the information which you accumulate about yourself, but it is most helpful (and time saving) to have readily available all the data which you will need.

These and other records which you will be keeping are for your own private use only. If they are to be truly effective then it is important that you are entirely honest with yourself when compiling them; don't omit an item because it makes you uncomfortable to think about it, or you wish that it hadn't happened. In the formal letter and application for a job you will, quite naturally, wish to emphasise those qualities, qualifications and experiences which will enhance your chances and therefore you might choose to lay stress on certain facts and deal more vaguely with others. This is sensible and quite legitimate and is practised by most candidates; however, it does not reduce the necessity of having a full, detailed and totally honest account in your master file.

The material in your Personal History file will not only help you when filling in application forms or compiling your Curriculum Vitae (account of your previous career), it will also be invaluable in focusing your attention on those items which are relevant to the job on offer. It will also help you think about the most positive way you can present the facts relating to the areas where you consider yourself to be weakest.

The Personal History file which you will compile for your own use is nothing more than a list — a detailed and accurate list under selected headings which you will constantly review and update. This list will allow you to think about what you have to offer; it will highlight areas of strength (and should also indicate weaknesses), and will give you a basis from which to measure your attributes against the apparent needs of any organisation which is trying to fill a post.

As previously stated, you will probably never need to use all the information which you accumulate in your Personal History file when making any one application, and since each application for a position must be aimed at getting you that one specific job, it may be that you will seldom find yourself making identical applications for different posts.

There is one further benefit which is gained from the maintenance of records of your Personal History — there are some interview situations where you may feel yourself to be under some pressure (perhaps deliberately contrived by the interviewer) and questions are coming thick and fast. Either as a result of threatening questions or because of the stressful circumstances a candidate can discover, to his horror, that he has dried up and cannot think of what to say next. A similar reaction can be seen occasionally on television when the person on camera (usually someone with little experience of TV work) freezes and obviously can't think of anything to say.

Working routinely on your Personal History file — together with other preparation which will be explained later — will ensure that, almost without you being aware that you have had to think about the question, the answer you are searching for is readily available.

Take care to be as detailed as possible when completing the Personal History and do remember to be completely candid with yourself. Most of the headings in the Personal History file shown on pages 14–15 are self-explanatory, but it will be helpful to look at the significance of two of them:

Family background   A small number of employers may show an interest in your family and lifestyle, whether or not you welcome such an interest, in the hope that this will give them some further indication of your suitability for the job under consideration.

Significant operation of employer, etc   If, during any period of work in the past, your employer was engaged in any project which might have a bearing on something you could be involved in with future employers, then this should be noted, particularly if you were directly involved at the time. Experience is a marvellous teacher, and any new skills you have had to acquire in the course of your work should be noted.

Although the facts outlined in your Personal History file relate to matters where you have, of course, personal knowledge, you may find that it is necessary to return and add items from time to time.

YOUR PERSONAL HISTORY FILE

PERSONAL

Name:

Date of birth: Place of birth:

Address: Nationality:

Telephone: Home: Business:

Marital status: Children (names
                                        and dates of birth):

National Insurance No: Current Driving
                                        Licence:

Religion:

Nationality: Passport No. and
                                        expiry date:

Family background   (e.g. lifestyle; social activities; parents'
occupations):

EDUCATION

Schools: From: To:
Colleges/Polytechnics/Universities, etc   From: To:

Participation in non-academic activities at school, college,
etc; offices held, details of interests and achievements (not
scholastic) whilst receiving full-time or part-time education:

Further Education: Full-time / Part-time

                                        From: To:

Examinations passed (description and
details)   Grade: Date:

TRAINING (includes training at work)

Formal: Description: Where: When:

Informal: Description: Where: When:

Qualifications obtained:

OTHER SKILLS

(E.g. fluency in foreign language, in training techniques; any specialised knowledge; membership of any job-related organisations, including posts held.)

H. M. FORCES

Service: Date joined: Where served:

Rank on discharge: Date released:

Training and experience (including specialised skills):

EMPLOYMENT HISTORY

Most recent job listed first (include temporary jobs when receiving full time education).

Each job: Dates started and   Job title:
                       finished:

                       Summary of   Skills required:
                       responsibilities:

                       Principal   Promotions
                       accomplishments: achieved:

                       Salary: Reason for leaving:

                       Any significant operation of employer
                       during your time:

                       Any new skill acquired:

LEISURE INTERESTS

Participation in sporting activities; membership of clubs and other organisations; community involvements; hobbies, etc.

Job application portfolio

The Personal History file will become the first of a small number of documents which you should keep in your job application portfolio. Keep these important records together (a ring binder is a good method to use) and they will form the basis of your attack on the job market.

These records, together with the advice and techniques set out in these pages, will ensure that your efforts meet with far more success than you would have thought possible.

4 ASSESSING YOUR PERSONAL QUALITIES

Whilst considering the jobs which are available and identifying those where you have the best chance of being selected it is most helpful to have made some evaluation of your own attributes, strengths and weaknesses.

When you have a realistic idea of your standing then you are in a much better position to identify those jobs where you are likely to perform well and where your applications will have a real chance of success.

Score from 1–10

Below are listed your most important characteristics and accomplishments. Consider each heading and associated comments and, as objectively as you can, score yourself from 1 (weakest) to 10 (strongest) in every section, remembering what the ideal employer will be looking for. Record your scores in the boxes provided. If this exercise is to be of real value it is important that you take a close and insightful look at yourself, sparing no pain!

Add this self-assessment record — together with your personal ratings — to your job application portfolio.

Background

Social level (as demonstrated by interests, circle of friends, mode of speech, parents' occupation, home circumstances) are of interest to some interviewers but not to others, depending upon the nature of the post on offer and the employer's personal preferences. Have relatives worked for the company now advertising or in similar work? This can sometimes be a distinct advantage, since it may be considered that this is evidence of some commitment to the job and, perhaps, some inherited family skill.

Consider your family composition and lifestyle, personal interests and hobbies.

Age

To some employers applicants who are younger than 25 will not have enough experience or, if over 50, might be considered likely to be too rigid in outlook, no longer energetic and to have lost their ambition. Looking at some advertisements one could be forgiven for thinking that employers only want staff who are aged between 25 and 35 years of age! The actual scene is far different from this, but it is a fact that if you are at the lower end of the age range for employment, or if you have less than 15 or 20 years of employment ahead of you, then there are special considerations which apply (which will be dealt with more fully later).

Health and personal appearance

A history of poor health or record of long absences from work due to sickness will be a disadvantage to a candidate, particularly if the illness is job related.

Personal appearance is important. Are you too fat or do you look frail? Do you appear alert or are you apathetic? Will you go into the interview coughing or sweating? Are you alert and energetic in appearance or do you look as if you might collapse any minute? Are you well groomed? These are all factors which are likely to influence most interviewers, whether they would admit to it or not.

Intelligence

How bright are you? Do you believe that you can cope with the demands which will be made of you in a new job? If you are expected to look imaginatively at long-standing problems and devise new ways of solving them would you be able to manage? Are you quick at learning and could you cope with training courses, especially if they are on subjects which are unfamiliar to you?

Of course, the possession of a superior intelligence is no guarantee that a person will shine at work; intelligence does not necessarily indicate the possession of wisdom. There are some people who are so devastatingly bright that it inhibits their colleagues, others who are quite unable to apply their talents in a meaningful way.

Qualifications

Do you have adequate qualifications which would indicate a good general education; i.e. what examinations did you pass at school, college or university? Have you had any success in gaining technical or professional qualifications? How extensive is your formal and informal training?

Generally speaking, the more specialised or important the jobs the less weight will be given to earlier general attainments and more confidence will be shown in qualifications in the particular area of interest which has relevance to the employer's business.

On the other hand, an employer may be looking for a junior member of staff who will be starting near the bottom in his business, but who might be expected to learn and mature so that he eventually merits promotion. In these circumstances he would look for evidence of a good basic education because a) there would be a sound foundation on which to build and b) it would indicate that the person concerned was probably intelligent enough to tackle the tasks and training with which he will be confronted in his new post.

Work experience

At one time it was considered to be an asset to have a record of long employment with one employer. Times have changed, however, and employers like to see candidates for jobs who can demonstrate a variety of experience in their employment history.

They would consider that a person who has made a success of previous posts not too dissimilar to the one on offer would bring to his job a wider outlook which would be reflected in maturity and flair.

A record of too frequent job changes, on the other hand, might be taken as an indication of incompetence at work, or evidence of some difficulties in relationships with colleagues, unless convincing reasons could be given for this history.

Skills and aptitudes

As demonstrated by work experience, training, qualifications and outside interests. If the skills that have been acquired over the years are within a very narrow and specialised field, then this would have a restricting effect on the jobs which might be available. Alternatively, your past record might indicate a wide general experience without the responsibility for specific tasks which would have given specialised knowledge. Assess the value of your experience to potential employers.

Expertise can be acquired outside the work situation and aptitudes are also developed in pursuing personal interests; don't forget to consider whether or not you have skills which are not directly related to past employment but which might be of interest to future employers.

Can you state that you are hard working, reliable, enterprising and imaginative and prove this from your past record — any employer would be interested in appointing staff with these qualities.

Written communication skills

The ability to write so that you make your point clearly and without unnecessary frills is an asset. This can be demonstrated in your letter of application and Curriculum Vitae.

Good handwriting might be expected in junior clerical posts, for example, but would not be considered so important in more technical jobs. The higher the status of the post, the less important is handwriting (unless it is so poor that no-one else can decipher it).

Verbal communication skills

An articulate and fluent interviewee will more easily impress (unless he appears too "slick"). The ability to speak clearly and convincingly on subjects in your area of interest is a very useful asset not only at interview, but also in most work situations.

Enthusiasm

Employers expect applicants to show keenness and enthusiasm for the position they are seeking. It is also helpful, in most circumstances, to convince them that their potential employee has energy, staying power, for management jobs the ability to motivate his fellow workers, and is able to work under pressure. If positions of some importance and power are being sought then it is helpful to have the ability to assert oneself if necessary (without any aggression).

Ambition

This is usually considered to be a desirable quality, but it can occasionally get out of control. There are some people who, it would appear, are willing to sacrifice almost anything if they can achieve their goal. It is possible to identify a few people like this where a close scrutiny of their lives will often reveal that the price they have paid for their status is a series of ruined relationships and the development of a single-minded outlook which seems to exclude any enjoyment of life.

It is not a fault to be ambitious. Certainly most employers would welcome an indication that candidates want to get on since this implies that they are willing to work for their promotion. Don't overdo it at interview, however. It is not advisable to answer the question "what position would you see yourself having in five years time?" by "Yours, Sir!"

Consider your motivation; how keen are you to make a success of your career? Are you prepared to sacrifice some immediate pleasures to achieve your goal?

Maturity

This is not always guaranteed by age. Can you demonstrate maturity of outlook and vision, rather rare and sought-after qualities? All of us retain some childish attitudes in our make-up, but do you, by and large, have a responsible outlook on life? Are you able to take a cool, calm look at a situation and make an objective judgement? Do you have confidence in that judgement once it is made? Are you self-sufficient?

If you are aiming for a job with considerable responsibility then these are important factors.

Relationships

Are you able to form profitable relationships with your colleagues? Are you easy to get along with, or a solitary person?

Employers will be keen to make some judgement about how you will fit into their establishment; how you will relate to your equals, to your superiors and to those subordinate to you. Your manner at interview and past record are important here.

Flexibility

How easy to do you find it to adjust to new situations and methods? Are you quick to learn and can you "think on your feet"?

Most employers look for flexibility of outlook in their workers. A rigid, old-fashioned employee who believes that everything was better "in the good old days" would generally be considered a liability. On the other hand, someone who thought that none of the old methods (which have been tested by time) have any merit would be thought to be too superficial in approach.

With so many new techniques and changes of approach in almost every sphere of employment there are now a wide range of training opportunities available to staff; by these means employers can make the very best use of their workforce. An employee who could not benefit from training schemes would not be favourably regarded.

Sense of humour

A well-developed sense of humour is an asset, so long as it is used in appropriate situations and is not offensive. If you are sufficiently at ease to raise a smile in the interview situation then this would certainly help your presentation.

Leadership

How important it is to display or give evidence of leadership qualities depends upon the type of job which is offered, or the future prospects which are sought. Generally speaking, it would be in the interviewee's favour if it could be demonstrated that he or she possessed the capacity to lead; but not, of course, by arrogant or dogmatic methods, leading others merely by giving instructions.

Aim not so much to be "pushy", as to have people follow your example or do as you suggest because they are persuaded that this is to their advantage. The successful leader does not achieve his objective by dominating others; although he may assert his authority at times he is not insensitive to the feelings of others.

Think of situations where you have shown that you have leadership qualities or potential — you may have the chance to illustrate your strengths when being interviewed.

Personality

Are you out-going or introverted? Tense or calm? Have you a warm or cold manner? Are you cheerful or pessimistic? Full of fun or humourless? Normal people usually have some irrational fears and phobias tucked away and anxieties which they struggle to hide, but would it be true to describe you as a well-balanced individual, using your aggression in an acceptable way and generally feeling at ease with yourself?

How do you cope with stress? A calm, unflustered applicant always impresses, although most employers will make allowances. It is, after all, natural to show some tension in an interview situation.

5 HOW TO IMPROVE YOUR ASSETS

Your self-assessment scores probably underline deficiencies which you were already aware of, and you will have found that you are not rated as highly as you would wish in some areas. Do not despair — perfection is a state that not one of us achieves and every other person in a similar position to yourself wishes that he/she were better in some aspect of his/her presentation.

Although there is a limit to everyone's capacity for change, we seldom even approach that limit and there is absolutely no doubt that most of us can improve substantially upon what we have to offer. How much we can improve our standing depends, to a large extent, on how much effort and perseverance we are prepared to devote to the task. Below are some practical suggestions.

Health

There is a very real connection between how fit we are and our appearance, attitudes and energy (all factors very relevant to the job-seeker). If you can improve your physical wellbeing, say by more attention to diet and planned exercise, then you will not only do better in your search for the right job, you are likely to look more presentable when you meet your interviewer.

Qualifications

There are now numerous ways of obtaining additional and relevant qualifications, even for a person currently in full-time employment, and the fact that it may be a long time since you were involved in any formal learning should not deter you — there are countless examples of mature people passing examinations and learning new skills.

If more training or an academic qualification would help your search, then think seriously about the opportunities which are available. There is a very useful spin-off if you embark on any learning programme; the more you are required to use your mental capacities then the more alert you become and therefore more likely to improve your chance of landing the job you want.

Writing skills

Clear handwriting is certainly not going to lessen your chances, although an illegible scrawl could! Consider the case of an employer who has received 30 applications for a job. He has decided that he does not want to interview more than five candidates and reads through each application to determine which are worthy of interview. Since almost every person who has this sort of decision-making role has many other demands on his or her time, they are not going to spend more than a minute or two on each application at this stage and if one is so badly written that it is hardly decipherable then that application will almost certainly be rejected.

Unless you are quite sure that, because of the type of post you are after, your handwriting technique is irrelevant, then you would be well advised to make sure that your writing is clear. If it is very poor, then a little serious practice can soon bring it up to standard. You will be advised later that application forms and C.V.s should be typed or printed, but some employers like to see handwritten applications (or the short accompanying letter might be better handwritten), and it would be a pity to jeopardise future endeavours by neglecting something as simple as this.

No matter what you have to offer in your written application the reader's judgement will be influenced by the clarity of your expression and, if you are invited for interview, your success might well depend upon how convincingly you can sell yourself and your ideas. Few people have nothing to learn in these areas, and I suggest that you give serious thought to ways and means of improving your written work — and becoming a more effective speaker.

If you believe that you are unable to make the most of what you are offering when you write for a job, then perhaps you should consider how you can improve your written English and, accordingly, your application. Wherever you live you are likely to find classes available, often on a part-time or evening basis, which can be of tremendous value; these courses might be vocational and lead to a recognised qualificaton, or they can be less structured, shorter, and aimed at meeting the needs of a mixed group of adults who are interested in improving their skills in presenting the written word. The local library will usually have details of what is available in the district or the local education authority will be able to point you in the right direction. There are also a number of good books available on letter-writing. Well chosen words which are clearly expressed go a very long way in convincing the readers that they want to hear more.

Verbal skills

It is well within the capabilities of most people to make remarkable progress in their style and manner of speech; this depends to a large extent upon confidence in oneself and practice in self expression. The more practice you have, the better you become — the better you perform, the more confident you are when the next opportunity presents itself.

How do you become more proficient in speaking? Again, it is possible to find courses in this specific subject which lead to some formal recognition or there are usually shorter courses available which could meet your needs.

There are, however, other ways of becoming a better speaker. Why not look around your area and see what organisations exist which operate in spheres where you have an interest, and where members are expected to use reasoned argument and debate in the general business of the group. It could be related to some hobby you have, or around subjects where you have strong feelings, e.g. conservation of the environment or providing help for deprived members of the community. Join the organisation, perhaps accept some office or responsibility, and take every opportunity of speaking to your fellow members, either individually or as a group, and you will be surprised how your speaking performance starts to improve, as will your prospects of success in your hunt for a job.

Quite apart from the direct advantages of improving your application and making more impact at the interview, you will find that, if you do cultivate an additional interest as suggested, mention of this fact when you are seeking work could impress the employer and be to your advantage. Also, involvement in something quite different — together with the stimulation of new friendships and fresh goals — will go a long way to helping you feel more alert and in control of your own destiny. This can be most important if you happen to be unemployed or in a post where you have little interest, no excitement and slender chances of promotion.

6 WHAT DO YOU WANT FROM A JOB?

Some people are quite clear about what they are seeking; others are not so sure. If you have little idea what sort of job you want because you haven't taken the trouble to think it through, then how can you reasonably expect to get a job where you can do well and which meets most of your current needs and future plans?

For people who have some uncertainty it is helpful to look at what you should be aiming for in your next job. Examine the headings in the list and make a note of the importance to you of the factors listed. Having looked at the list and decided on the relative importance of the various factors (adding any others which you believe are appropriate), make a written note of your conclusions and add this to your job application portfolio.

Your Job Requirements

Location: Must the work be in your present locality or are you prepared to move?

Environment: Do you prefer to work indoors or outdoors — a desk job or one with more mobility? With others, or would you rather work alone?

Career: Are you starting a new career or continuing your existing occupation?

Status: This is important to some people, of less significance to others. There is usually (but not always) a link between how the post is regarded by the public and the salary that the position attracts.

Salary: How important is a high income? A low starting salary does not mean that it cannot improve when you demonstrate your merit.

Prospects:	Is it security you are after or can you tolerate some uncertainty in the future? Is it essential that the job offers the possibility of promotion?
Purposeful:	Do you want to work in a field which benefits others?
Challenge:	Do you want a challenging post or one where you are not extended? Would you be content with routine, repetitive work or would you rather have an interesting and more demanding role?
Pressure:	Could you cope with working under pressure? Would you be willing to work after normal working hours and to take work home?
Dependence:	Would you be content to work under supervision or would you rather have independence?
Responsibility:	Is a responsible position sought?
Supervisory:	Would you want a job where you were answerable for others? Could you exercise control and lead other workers? How would you cope with the isolation from your colleagues which can often be part of such a position?
Job satisfaction:	How important is this?
Family:	Consider the wishes of your family. The support of your immediate family in your endeavours can be of tremendous value. To what extent will their lives be affected by your decisions?
Future career:	Define a) your short-term objectives; and b) your long-term objectives.

How it works

To illustrate the practical application of the job requirements list, it will be helpful to look at the situation of a person who is thinking about a job change.

Mrs. B is a woman in her early thirties with a son of 12. Some ten years ago, the family moved to the area when her husband was promoted by his firm to take charge of the branch office. They later split up and she is now the sole breadwinner.

She has worked for her present employer, a family firm of shoe manufacturers, for seven years starting as a short-hand typist and quickly advancing to her present post of private secretary to the Managing Director. Not only is she required to be proficient in the usual secretarial duties, over the past three or four years she has also been given additional responsibilities which in a larger organisation would be performed by an office manager and administrators. Considering her demanding role she is not well paid, and there seems no prospect of advancement.

In contemplating her future, Mrs. B feels that she would like a job which makes more use of her talents and offers a better future; she would also like to live nearer to her parents and many of her old friends.

Going through her job requirements list, Mrs. B would note in particular that the following categories would be the most important to her in her search for a more suitable job: location; career; salary/prospects; challenge; responsibility; job satisfaction; and, probably the most important of all, family circumstances. Having noted the relevance of these factors to her situation, she can then realistically measure each available job in her field against her requirements.

7 JOBS FOR ALL

Whether you're a school leaver, a member of the long-term unemployed, a mature job seeker, or a woman, certain basic principles and attitudes apply to all categories.

The school leaver

Much of what follows in this book is as important for school leavers as for any other group with more job experience. People who are thinking about their first job after finishing full-time education are in a unique position, however, and it will be helpful for anyone in this category to consider the following points.

Before you leave school   Take the trouble to discuss your future with appropriate teaching staff and career advisers before you leave school. Don't neglect to consult your parents, although it is likely that they will find it hard to be objective about your career and capabilities.

If representatives of employers or vocations speak at school meetings then try to attend. Help yourself to the brochures and leaflets that are often available at such meetings, and if there is someone there talking about work in which you are interested, have a private word with him or her after the meeting — even if no immediate opportunity can be put your way, there is the possibility that your name will be noted for the future. In your last year the school will sometimes arrange visits to local employers; go along, and follow up anything that excites your interest.

If you believe that you know what you want to do when you leave school, then try to speak to someone who works in that field and find out as much as you can about what is entailed in the job, what qualifications are needed, and which skills and qualities are likely to be required. If you think you fall short of the minimum requirements, then consider how you can acquire them.

Sometimes employers make enquiries at schools when looking to fill vacancies; find out at the school office if there has been any such approach. Some schools have job placement schemes for final-year pupils or, if you show enough keenness, they might even make special arrangements for you, which could lead to a job.

References will probably be sought from your Head Teacher before an employer offers you a job. Even though you may not have been brilliant at school your teachers will be keen to see you make a success of your life; try to talk to someone in authority about your future before you leave school.

You may be able to claim some academic success at school, but how is the employer to know that this will be of practical value to him? Although you may have little or nothing in the way of work experience, don't hesitate to draw a prospective employer's attention to any activities you have pursued which might show him that you have capabilities and talents which could be used at work.

Taking stock   In times when work is hard to find, many school leavers are half defeated before they start their search for a job; they know of so many of their contemporaries who haven't got a job after months (or even years) of unemployment and they regularly see in the daily paper or on TV that jobs are in scarce supply. When they finally say goodbye to school they are already resigned to being out of work for a long time. If you have the determination to look for a job and use the methods set out in this book, then you will have a head start over all those who are half beaten before they start.

You will not be short of advice, both from family and friends. By all means listen to what they say, but remember it is your future and no one else's. So make your own decisions.

Making a start   Many jobs are won by school leavers making personal application to employers, either by turning up within a short time of seeing an advertisement, by appointment after telephoning or even by arriving on his doorstep on the chance that there is something available. The hard work involved in making the effort to visit potential employers can be very productive if you stick at it. There is often less formality in the process of your first appointment than there is likely to be later, but do remember that the employer begins to make an assessment of you as soon as he speaks to you or sees you, so be prepared.

You will probably feel some anxiety at this stage; how do you choose the job that is right for you? Won't the wrong choice jeopardise your whole future? Remember that you are not making an irrevocable decision — most people change their jobs many times throughout their working life. Even if you find that the job you have got is not to your liking, do try to do the work as well as you can; there is absolutely no point in being half-hearted in your efforts. If you are determined to change your job then it is usually sensible to wait until you are offered another one before giving in your notice.

Congratulations! You've got your first job   After you have settled down, take a cool look at your position and your prospects. Perhaps further qualifications would help; if so then look at the opportunities available. It is often easier to study when young, since the older you are the longer it takes to re-acquire the study habit. It is a surprising fact that a large number of people seem to discover a taste for academic work only after they have left school and are able to appreciate, for the first time, the real value of knowledge.

Long-term unemployed

In recent years unemployment has become a very real phenomenon in many industrialised countries. There are, of course, a number of reasons for this, not least of which are the change of emphasis from traditional industries which were labour intensive and the increasing use of new technology.

Employers have come to expect their workers to be flexible in their thinking and ready to adopt new ideas or learn new skills. There is more prominence given than ever before to training and redevelopment schemes within the employing organisations.

It is true, of course, that with the increase in unemployment there are fewer jobs available. Consider, however, the other side of the coin: employers are obliged to become more efficient in order to survive; they are very keen, therefore, to spend their available money as wisely as possible and are on the lookout for good value when they appoint staff. Careful preparation and presentation on your part can convince them that you are a worthwhile bargain.

Attitude   The days are long gone when "unemployed" was considered to mean either unemployable or lazy; most people out of work are in this situation through no fault of their own. If you are in this group then rid yourself of any feeling of guilt or unworthiness and set about the business of finding suitable work; job-seeking can be interesting and pleasurable if you set about the task in a sensible and organised manner.

Your attitude will affect your job-hunting performance. No one is impressed by a pessimist and your feelings will tend to creep through and influence your presentation.

It is not easy to remain optimistic when unemployed. You may recall that Charles Dickens made Mr. Micawber an optimist who was forever making plans "in case anything turned up"; but although improvident he went to some trouble to find himself a situation, and was eventually successful. Optimism can grow as you become more competent with job applications and more convincing at interview; you will begin to sense that it can only be a matter of time before you succeed. Remind yourself that even in difficult times there are many jobs available — workers are retiring or moving, new businesses are being created, established concerns are expanding, more re-training schemes are becoming available.

Strategy If you are unemployed it is important to keep busy, even if most of your time is spent pursuing some hobby or interest you had little time for in the past. Make enquiries about the possibility of learning new skills.

Not only will this help to pass the time pleasantly and keep you feeling (and looking) alert, but also potential employers will be interested to hear that you have not just been waiting for "something to turn up".

Establish a routine in your job-seeking as advised throughout this book. Also, try to share your problems and get support and practical help from interested friends, from family or from a self-help group like a Job Club.

It is easier to get a job when you are employed. Consider, therefore, taking work that, whilst not exactly what you would want, might be a stepping stone to something better. Again, don't refuse opportunities for temporary work until you have thought about it carefully. Apart from the obvious advantages of more income and a better base for your serious job search, a temporary job can be a source of useful contacts, a chance to brush up old skills or acquire new ones and, if you impress your employer, there may be the possibility of permanent work with him in the future.

The mature job-seeker

Some individuals are on the lookout for better jobs throughout most of their careers, and a healthy desire for advancement is usually encouraged by go-ahead employers.

Leaving aside those people who are trying to take a step up the ladder, there are a multitude of reasons why older people look for jobs. They may have decided that it is no longer enough to feel "comfortable" in their jobs and believe they could do better. It may be that they have become more and more disenchanted in their work situation; they may have been passed over for promotion; the old values may seem to be disappearing, together with well-tested methods and good fellowship; there may be a hint of redundancy in the air. Many jobs disappear due to the reorganisation, takeover or collapse of established concerns.

Whatever the reason, many people who are looking for jobs in middle life are aware of a sense of failure, although the cause of their circumstances may have been quite beyond their control. This, together with the frustration caused by unsuccessful attempts to find a suitable job, can make this period a very unhappy one.

Taking stock   If you are an older person in the position of seeking a new job then take the trouble to examine your situation carefully. Don't discount entirely the prospect of a change of career; in these days it is not uncommon for people to re-train more than once during their working life. Ask yourself if you are sufficiently motivated and flexible enough to make a new start.

Do you know anyone who might help in your search, perhaps by way of introduction to someone on the lookout for new staff?

Whilst it is true that some organisations will be looking for relatively young employees where they feel they are more likely to find new ideas and a dynamic approach to a task, there are many who will value the qualities that an older person can offer: reliability, well-tested skills, the knack of remaining calm when under pressure, a mature outlook and judgement based upon years of experience. These are all attributes which are held in high esteem. Take every opportunity to remind employers that you have very valuable assets to offer.

Women

Although the position is slowly improving, women can sometimes be at a disadvantage when applying for jobs. This can be due to the prejudice of employers (who are usually men), and sometimes because of the attitude of women themselves, who won't rebel against the conventional view of what sort of job is suitable for a woman, or go along with the view held by some men that women do not usually possess attributes like assertiveness, leadership potential or drive which are needed in some jobs. Also of significance is the widely-held belief that women are in some ways less dependable (e.g. it is said they will have more time off work due to sickness than men, or will stay off to look after their children, or will leave because of pregnancy).

Women can, to some extent, blame their own past attitudes (some of which still linger on) for difficulties they may meet — many have regarded work as the stop-gap between leaving school and getting married; some have subscribed to the philosophy that women should "keep their place" and that many jobs are "men's work" — yet there are now countless examples of women working in what had traditionally been regarded as exclusively male preserves (e.g. lorry drivers, plumbers, airline pilots, mechanics).

Statistics which show that the average male worker earns far more than the average female will highlight this discrepancy because there are far more men in high positions (with high salaries) than there are women, and this distorts the picture. If the higher posts are excluded from any such survey, then the difference in earnings is far less marked.

Strategy Any woman exploring the job market would be well advised to remember that the employers' representatives might subscribe to some of the opinions set out above. In completing the written application and in preparing for interview she should consider how these out-dated arguments might be answered. It could be said, for instance, that a woman is less likely to change her job for career purposes; that the presence of a woman in a room full of men will have an uplifting effect on morale, and that a woman's point of view can often be very helpful.

It can be argued that it is unfair to ask a female candidate what arrangements she would make to care for her children when male candidates with children are never asked this question. She can, of course, take exception to this discrimination and challenge the interviewer; this will hardly endear her to him, however, and will almost certainly reduce her chances of appointment. A more positive answer would be one that shows she has thought this through, particularly if her partner is involved in the projected arrangements.

Sometimes the position is that a woman is looking for work after a long spell at home raising a family; she is likely to be out of touch with the latest techniques and has lost the habit of working to a strictly controlled schedule. In this position she can remind the employer that in looking after her family she did more than clean the house and make meals; she was required to engage in forward planning, in budgeting, in making the best possible use of close relationships and in being a guide and support to other members of the group (all attributes which are used in the more formal work setting).

If a return to work is contemplated it might be useful to become involved in community activities, in fund raising or even in part-time work. All these will help to get into the swing of things again and can be mentioned when applying for full-time work.

8 THE SEARCH FOR VACANCIES

Whatever your personal circumstances, remember that although there is fierce competition for jobs, there are many thousands of opportunities every week and the more competently you set about seeking a new post, the better chance you have of success.

How urgent is your quest for a job?

Your personal situation will influence your reply. If you have been unemployed for some time or made redundant you may feel that it is essential to find work as soon as possible; if you are no longer young then you are conscious that time is not on your side and the older you are, the harder it will become to convince employers to appoint you.

In these situations you may believe that any job is better than none, and certainly it may be easier to get the job of your choice if you are already working than otherwise. However, employers are often reluctant to appoint a person to a job which is obviously well below his or her capabilities since they suspect that he/she will regard this as a stop-gap and the first opportunity will be taken to move to something better, leaving the employer with the same job to fill again, having wasted time in training a new employee. If you are in this situation then you may either have to persuade the employer that you are, in fact, changing direction and willing to start in a modest position from which you hope to be promoted or, on the other hand, put your cards on the table but undertake to stay in the job an agreed minimum time.

You may, of course, be in employment but keen to change your job for something better, or perhaps something different, in which case urgency need not be a factor.

Plan your attack

There is an argument sometimes advanced that the job-hunter should send off as many applications as possible. The theory being that if, say, applicants are invited to just one interview for every 50 applications they make and one offer of employment is made for every ten interviews, then it follows that if a person makes 500 applications he/she will, by the law of averages, get a job. Unfortunately a reasoned argument such as this does not always work out in practice — and think of the devastating effect on your morale of hundreds of rejections!

Although it is certainly advisable to apply for jobs which appeal to you and where you meet, say, 60 per cent rather than all of the specified requirements, it is not sensible to apply for jobs where there is no prospect of consideration. For example, if a firm seeking a legal assistant asks for applications from persons who are practising law or who possess a degree in law, then it is quite futile to apply if all you can offer is examination success in woodwork! Be realistic in your endeavours.

Establish a routine. The careful, methodical approach is best and can be enjoyable if tackled in the right spirit. There is a clear relationship between the time spent in preparing and making applications and the success you can expect.

Business and social acquaintances

Many jobs are filled after the posts have been advertised and interested parties invited to apply. It is a surprise to many people to learn, however, that a very large number of vacancies are filled without going through these formalities; sometimes even when the job has been advertised and interviews held (because company policy required these procedures), the result was a foregone conclusion since the decision had been made beforehand. Whilst we might deplore these tactics you should recognise that they exist.

Consider whether or not any of your friends, acquaintances or colleagues can assist you in your search. Do they know people who work in key positions in commerce, industry or the public sector, and if so could they arrange an introduction? Do you yourself know any such person who might welcome a direct approach?

Perhaps you should make more effort to get to know the people who make decisions about engaging staff: attend meetings, functions and other events connected with the field in which you have an interest and where you will meet influential people; very useful contacts can be made by these means. Make it your business to speak to selected individuals if possible and, if you consider it fitting, mention your interest in a new appointment.

Don't forget to write (or telephone) and thank anyone who has helped you.

One can understand why some employers feel happier giving a job to someone whom they know or who is recommended by a trusted colleague, since they believe that this method is less of a gamble than any formal procedure where a great deal has to be taken at face value.

Unsolicited approaches

Many jobs are awarded to people who make direct contact with employers, sometimes without even the formality of any prior invitation to interview.

It is certainly possible, with most appointments, to increase your chances of selection by making informal approaches to companies and organisations who are not advertising for staff. Many posts never appear on the open market and this may be the only way to compete for these jobs. Also, it may be possible to anticipate an advertisement and therefore ensure that your name is noticed as someone who is "on the ball". By these means you can cash in on the predicament of employers who want replacement staff quickly and would prefer not to have to wait for the inevitable delay involved when advertising.

Do make sure that you keep yourself up to date with what is happening in your field; keep abreast of the news — if yours is the only enquiry relating to job opportunities after news has broken of expansion of work in an organisation then you will have a head start.

Look up addresses, telephone numbers and other relevant details of employers in your local library, trade directories, Chambers of Commerce or at trade shows. Information about such matters as profitability, assets, and staff employed is readily available if you are prepared to search.

If you still have uncertainty about a career then any good reference library will have publications which will give detailed information about a whole range of occupations, including such matters as environment, pay and conditions, opportunities, entry requirements and training.

Guidance will be given in subsequent pages on the form and phrasing of letters written "on spec." in the hope of arousing the interest of prospective employers.

Advertised vacancies

The obvious sources of information about available jobs, and one which you must not neglect, are the Vacancies and Appointments sections of newspapers and specialist periodicals.

Find out which national newspapers advertise the type of post which you are aiming for, and ensure that you get the chance to look through them regularly. Local newspapers always have a section devoted to offers of employment, and should not be neglected even if you believe it unlikely that the type of work you are seeking will be advertised there. Often there is one particular day of the week when more space is devoted to job opportunities and this should make your search easier to organise.

Specialist journals offer a rich variety of posts waiting to be filled, and you should ensure that you see the appropriate magazine on a regular basis, either by placing an order with your news agent or enquiring if it can be seen at your local library.

It may be that you are unsure which particular periodical you should read regularly since there often appears such a wide variety of choice. Use the facilities of your local library where you will almost certainly find directories which not only list all the newspapers and periodicals, but also give details like frequency of distribution, price, circulation figures and number of Vacancy Advertising pages (all of which have significance to job-seekers).

Self-advertisement

In their search for work, some people advertise their talents and availability for hire. Unless they have some special skill or facility to offer, however, this is likely to prove disappointing for them, and the more common this form of advertising becomes then the less response can be expected.

Employment agencies

There are many agencies offering services to both job-hunters and employers. They range from the local Job Centre service which lists jobs available in the locality, to Management Consultants and Executive Recruitment Agencies which specialise in posts for highly qualified or experienced executives.

Some of these organisations are government sponsored, some work for employers, who will usually pay a commission, whilst others employ and pay staff themselves, placing them with firms who pay a regular fee which is higher than the salary the worker receives, the agency retaining the difference. There are agencies which specialise in defined areas of employment, others in special groups (e.g. mature executives, former commissioned officers of the Armed Forces).

You can find, in the national papers which carry advertisements for the top jobs, specialist agencies who will help you find the position of your choice through the "unadvertised job market". Commercial agencies can be found which will offer vocational guidance. These organisations usually do not help in finding jobs but rather evaluate their clients' attributes and potential and give advice on, for instance, how to develop insight and improve job prospects. Private agencies such as these can be rather costly.

9 EVALUATING THE JOBS ON OFFER

Employers

It is most important that you know as much as possible about an employer when you are seriously considering working for him. The more you know about his reputation, prospects, methods, work environment and his record of staff management the better you are able to judge whether or not you would care to work for him. Additionally, when he discovers at interview that you are well informed about his organisation (and you should take the opportunity to make him aware of your knowledge), he will be suitably impressed. Use the sources already mentioned for your investigations and if it is possible to talk to an employee without jeopardising your application, then do so.

Is the employer in a small way of business or is it a large concern? A small organisation will probably have a friendly atmosphere with the emphasis on informality, although the impact of even one difficult person in authority can be considerable; there are likely to be fewer opportunities for training or promotion than with a larger company. In a large organisation there is likely to be some insistence on working by the rules and involvement with "red tape" might cause some frustration. Also, in a large company there is often the opportunity for a wide range of experience and in-service training, with brighter promotion prospects than a small firm can offer.

What does the job involve?

Consider carefully all the information you have about a job, whether from an advertisement or from some other source. Eliminate those posts which are unattractive on closer examination and those which, on reflection, offer little hope of success if you apply.

Read the advertisement carefully (or study the information you have, if from another source) and consider what you can reasonably assume that the work entails. If you are uncertain on some *fundamental* aspect of the duties or conditions of service, then contact the employer concerned and make polite enquiry from someone who can speak with some authority about the job on offer. If you are able to speak to the person who will be doing the interviewing, then usually so much the better, but you will have to make a careful judgement as to whether or not he/she is likely to be irritated by enquiries at this stage. An employer should welcome such an approach as evidence that a prospective candidate is thinking seriously about the post.

Box numbers Consider carefully before you respond to box numbers. If an organisation has any standing at all then it is unlikely to hide behind the anonymity of this form of advertising. Expect few replies if you apply to a box number.

---

a) **Secretary** required for our Bristol Office
Requirements 80 w.p.m. Shorthand; 40 w.p.m. Typing
Experience of Word Processing an advantage
Application Form & Job Description from —

---

b) **SALES ASSISTANT**

Very high earnings
potential for persons
with good sales ability
Apply in writing to —

---

c) **Assistant Manager c£20k + Benefits**

We are a dynamic Company with an exciting future on the lookout for the person who will lead an established sales and support team and deputise in the absence of the Manager.
The successful applicant will have a good academic record with experience in man-management. He or she will have demonstrated an ability for original thinking and problem solving.
Write, in confidence, with full career details to —

Evaluating advertisements

Let's assess the three typical advertisements shown opposite.

a) Since this advertiser is precise about the skills required then it is likely that they will want to see certificates to confirm that candidates have the necessary speeds. If you have one speed but not quite the other it may be worthwhile applying, but if you have neither then it could be a waste of time. Candidates will probably be given a shorthand and typing test.

The technique of word processing can be quickly learned, so if you say that you have no experience but are willing to learn this should be sufficient. There is no mention of audio typing — if you have experience of this you should say so.

Electronic typewriters are now used extensively. If you haven't used one of these machines then it would be sensible to get some practice, even if this means hiring one for a week.

b) You really need to know more about this job. "Very high earnings potential" sounds ominous; it is likely that all or nearly all of the wage will be commission, with constant pressure to increase sales! What are they selling?

c) c£20k + Benefits means that the salary is approximately £20,000 per annum and is negotiable around that figure; the benefits could be a company car, a non-contributary pension, expenses allowance, private health care or a number of other items which could substantially increase the real income.

Clearly, this employer is looking for a very competent, go-ahead individual who is right up to date in his/her thinking and style. Less importance will be placed on examination results than on evidence of success in the practice of the skills required; a record of past promotions or advancements would help.

Knowledge of the product(s) of the company may not be required if a candidate can show leadership qualities, encouraging past achievements and has some skill in the use of relationships.

Objectives

Having determined to your own satisfaction that you have a fair idea of what is on offer then, using the same headings as set out under Chapter 6, What do you want from a job?, make judgements about the job and compare your conclusions with the earlier assessment of your ideal goal (held in your job application file); the comparison should give you clear indications as to whether or not you should apply for this position.

What qualities will the successful applicant need?

Having thought carefully about the job, and perhaps having made further enquiries, you should know not only what the responsibilities of the post are, but also you should be in a position to assess what background, skills and qualities will be required to perform the duties adequately.

Your self-assessment record, which is in your job application portfolio (see Chapter 4), is a record of the ratings which you have given yourself in terms of qualifications, experience, skills, aptitudes and personal characteristics. Use the same list and method of scoring (1 to 10) and evaluate the likely requirements for the job under consideration.

Compare the marks you have awarded yourself with the marks you have given the job. You are now in a position to make some judgement about your suitability.

It is not likely that you will find, either when comparing the job offered with your ideal job, or looking at the correlation of your self-assessment ratings and the qualities required for the post, that there will be an exact "match" of markings — you should expect some deviation even if the job seems just to your liking.

If it is clear, however, when comparing notes on yourself and the job you would choose with the notes on the responsibilities and demands of the job under consideration, that there are wide and fundamental differences, then you would be well advised to think again about this particular vacancy.

10 APPLYING FOR THE JOB

The principal purpose when making the first approach is to arouse the interest of the employer and make him feel that he would like to hear more. In the formal written application he will require to be convinced that here is an applicant who appears to have relevant qualifications, experience and personal qualities, and who seems to be motivated to make a success of the job on offer. If his curiosity is further stimulated by an excellent presentation and an eager style — then so much the better.

By telephone

As mentioned earlier, it is sometimes worthwhile telephoning an employer when you believe that there is a possibility of a suitable vacancy coming up. Alternatively, it may be that the employer is seeking a telephone enquiry in the first instance, or you have decided that you should find out more about an advertised vacancy.

In any event, when you make a telephone call regarding a job there are some important considerations. Try to speak to a person of some influence in the organisation, preferably the person who will be interviewing or who will be making the appointment (the same person may have both roles), although you must remember that such people have many demands on their time and you will have to decide whether or not that person will be irritated by your enquiry. If you are phoning merely to have something clarified, then the interviewer's secretary is probably the person to approach.

Remember that from the moment of your first contact with the employer's representative he/she is forming some opinion of you; in effect, you have begun to make your application. You would usually have only a short conversation at this stage, often restricting yourself to discussing or enquiring about questions of fact.

Be certain in your own mind what it is you want to talk about and state your name and business clearly. It is sensible to make a note in advance of the questions you wish to ask and to have available by the telephone your job application portfolio containing your Personal History, together with any details of the job (or employer) you may know. Have a pen and paper handy so that you can make notes of what is said, and write out these notes immediately you have finished your conversation, adding them to any material you may have on the job under discussion.

Let us eavesdrop on the way a typical enquiry should be handled. There has been a feature article in the local newspaper on Herbert Lumpton & Son, the retail and wholesale booksellers, and it appears that a new contract they have secured will increase the turnover of the firm by more than 50 per cent:

"Hello, I am calling about the possibility of employment and I would like to speak to Mr. Smithson" (Mr. Smithson is the office manager and the enquirer has discovered that he is responsible for the engagement of office staff).

"Hello, Mr. Smithson speaking. Who is that please?"

"My name is Judith Hudson, Mr. Smithson. I read in yesterday's *Evening News* that Lumpton & Son will be increasing their business and may take on more staff. I'm phoning in the hope that you would allow me to apply for a post with you."

"Well, Miss Hudson, you are certainly quick off the mark. What sort of job are you looking for?"

"I have worked as a shorthand typist since I left school five years ago, and have some experience with audio typing, word processing and general office work. I would very much like to do similar work for you, if there is a chance."

"Let me have your address, Miss Hudson, and I will send you our standard Application Form. I hope to have the pleasure of meeting you in the near future."

This example is of a telephone conversation which lasted only one or two minutes, yet because the enquirer had taken the trouble to speak to the appropriate person and knew what she intended to speak about, that time was very well spent. She would be remembered by Mr. Smithson, and that short conversation could give her the edge over competitors with a similar background.

Uninvited approach by letter

As has been argued, serious consideration should be given in favourable circumstances to writing a letter of enquiry about the possibility of employment, even though the organisation in question is not currently advertising a vacancy.

Since the employer has not asked for this approach he may not welcome it and therefore you must be prepared for a relatively high failure rate. On the other hand, when your timing has proved just right you will have stolen a march on all the potential opposition and could well be regarded as a very worthy candidate, having shown that you possess initiative and imagination.

It is important to use the right style of approach in this situation. Try to find out the name and position of the person who is the decision-maker on employment issues and write to that person by name. The individual who will read your unsolicited letter will be in a position of responsibility (you hope) and will, therefore, have little time to spare on matters which they would consider unimportant.

Be brief, to the point — yet interesting. Do not expect that this busy person will take the time to go carefully through several pages of a letter (which has not been sought) in the expectation of finding a candidate for a vacancy which has not been made public.

At this stage, your enquiry should be limited to one page. Make sure that your name, address and telephone number are clearly written and that the correspondence is correctly addressed to the identified person, marking the envelope "Confidential". The letter must be designed to impress; use good-quality stationery. If you have enough confidence in your writing skills it can be handwritten (in black ink — in case it is photocopied); otherwise have it typed and sign your name clearly.

In the first paragraph explain simply why you are writing and describe the role which you feel you could fill. In the second (and possibly third) paragraph(s) outline the most relevant facts about yourself, and finally try to convince the reader that you are really interested in working for his organisation and that you have a lot to offer.

It would not be helpful to include a Curriculum Vitae with this first enquiry, although you would mention that a detailed C.V. is available whenever required.

The person reading your letter is committed to promoting the company's interests, not yours! He or she has to be convinced that you could be an asset to the employer and this belief will be encouraged if you are able to include in your letter of enquiry evidence that you are aware of what the employer does and that you have some knowledge of the firm's recent history and plans for the future.

In this — as in all applications — you are in the business of selling yourself. You must capture the attention of the employer's representative and convince that person, in a few short paragraphs, that it would be worthwhile spending valuable time, first in answering your enquiry, and later in interviewing you.

Example of a letter written "on spec"

Mr. Arthur E. Dunwood,
Personnel Manager,
Samuelson & Duffy, Ltd.,
Derengham,
Northamptonshire

83 Twentholm Avenue,
Sedgebury,
Berkshire,
SF3 4HO
Tel: Sedgebury (0413) 357

4th January, 1989

Dear Mr. Dunwood,

Within the next two months I shall be moving to Derengham with my parents and I am writing to you in the hope that I might be considered for a suitable post with Samuelson & Duffy.

Since I left full-time education some four years ago, where I had success at both "O" and "A" levels of the G.C.E. Examination, I have worked in the retail industry with a large multiple store, gaining promotion to a supervisory post last year.

I am keen to continue my career in the retail trade, and would welcome the opportunity to work for Samuelson & Duffy, a firm with a reputation for high standards of service and goods, and where there is a structured training programme with the possibility of earning promotion.

If you wish to have further details of my background I would be pleased to send particulars of my career history and could, of course, attend for interview if required.

Yours sincerely,

(James R. Destin)

Remember to keep a copy of your letter. If you are invited for interview then it is quite likely that you will be invited to develop some statement you made; re-read the letter before you keep your appointment.

Study carefully the example of an "on spec." letter given here but please understand that it and the above suggestions are guidelines only, albeit founded on important principles. There may be special circumstances relating to your own situation or to the prospective employer which may persuade you to adopt a rather different approach. So think the matter through carefully.

Application forms

It is becoming more common for employers to require job applicants to complete printed application forms. By these means it is possible to ensure that all candidates have supplied the basic written information thought to be required at the initial stage of selection. It is then relatively easy to make direct comparisons between the competitors.

There are disadvantages, however, in using application forms, both from the employers' and the applicants' point of view. It is usual, except where the most senior jobs are concerned, for these forms to be devised in such a way that they can be used by applicants for a wide variety of posts within the same organisation.

Since the background of people applying for quite dissimilar jobs is likely to have many points of difference, it follows that even if the correct questions are asked there is not always sufficient space available in particular sections of the form for a candidate to do him/herself justice. If the form is made extremely comprehensive, covering all the areas which might be relevant to any job likely to be offered, the form becomes very large and unwieldy and its value is diminished.

Whilst a Curriculum Vitae gives you the opportunity to present your candidacy in the most favourable manner, an application form allows no such latitude, and great care requires to be exercised in making your submission. Nevertheless, you must not send in a C.V. if a completed application form is expected.

Guidelines   You should have adequate information in your Personal History file to complete the form. If there is something missing, then update your Personal History records. The same principles apply as set out in Chapter 11, Compiling your Curriculum Vitae.

Restriction of space under certain headings may make it necessary for you to modify both the content and the style from how you would choose to complete the form. Ensure that you have dealt adequately with matters which you consider important for the job in question and, if necessary, deal more briefly with less critical items (e.g., if there is not enough space to give all the details of your past employment, then summarise your early work history and set out more fully your recent, and more relevant, job record).

If you believe that you cannot do yourself justice in the space available, then use an additional sheet of paper (drawing attention to this on the application form). Use this method sparingly.

Sometimes questions are asked which are totally inappropriate — resist the temptation to answer facetiously; simply write "not appropriate".

Take a photocopy of the application form when you receive it (then put the original to one side since you will want to keep it clean and relatively uncreased); use this for practice and as a copy of your submission; take the trouble to check carefully for omissions or spelling mistakes before filling in the original form.

Preferably, the form should be completed in typescript. If you believe that your handwriting is good enough then write your application, allowing enough space for what you want to say.

Covering letter

Whether returning a completed application form or sending a Curriculum Vitae it is advisable to enclose a covering letter, which should be short and businesslike. In the first paragraph you could state how you became aware of the vacancy. You might then say a little about yourself and, if you thought it appropriate, why you would like to work in the position which is about to be filled. The penultimate paragraph would advise that the completed form (or C.V.) is enclosed and you should then end the letter with a brief phrase expressing the hope that you will hear further from the addressee.

Sample Covering Letter

123 Roughton Avenue
Huntsville,
PW3 QR9
Tel: Huntsville 3651

Mr. H. Smithson,
Personnel Manager,
Herbert Swafdown and Co.,
Kingsberry Court,
Huntsville   17th February, 1989

Dear Mr. Smithson,

Appointment of Office Manager

I am interested in your advertisement of the above post in the *Huntsville Courier*. During the past eleven years I have been employed by three companies in positions of increasing responsibility relating to office practice and management. I have had experience in credit and stock control, the calculation and distribution of wages and salaries and liaison with sub-offices. Recently I have been given the authority to up-date and monitor office procedure and have been made responsible for the supervision of clerical staff.

The challenge offered by the advertised post is one which I would welcome. I believe that my past experience, together with my capacity for hard work and eagerness to make a success of this opportunity, would be an asset to the Company.

I am enclosing my Curriculum Vitae [or completed application form], and look forward to hearing from you in the near future.

Yours sincerely,

(Harold R. Robertson)

When a covering letter is specifically requested

On occasions you may receive an application form together with the request that it is completed and returned with a supporting letter.

In these circumstances you are clearly expected to elaborate upon what you have written on the form and it would not be adequate to send a short letter as in the example just given.

Before completing the application form you will have decided how to make the best use of the space available. Nevertheless, there may well be additional matters you would have liked to include, had there been more space; also you might have wished to deal more fully with one or two aspects of your submission (for example, whilst you will have given details of your employment record there may not have been enough space to point out the skills which have been acquired, your achievements or the improvements you have been able to effect). Make a note of all these items and include them in your supporting letter.

A letter of just a few paragraphs is less than is expected in support of an application when such a letter has been specifically requested. Take care, however, not to be too lengthy; a two-page submission is about right.

Having covered your background in the application form, you

are obviously expected to say something different in the letter, and a re-phrasing of the points you have already made would not be acceptable. As mentioned, you can include relevant items which were not anticipated by the questions on the form and you can elaborate upon answers where you did not have the opportunity to do yourself justice. If there is any factor in your personal history which you feel strengthens your claim to consideration, then take this chance to emphasise this.

Make sure there is a thread of optimism in your letter. Don't be afraid to say that you welcome the challenge of the post on offer with its attendant responsibilities and try to allow your enthusiasm to be reflected in the style of your writing. It could help your application if you were able to say something about your goals and aspirations, although you must take care not to give the impression that you would only use this appointment as a stepping stone to something better (unless by promotion within the same organisation).

Avoid using clichés and jargon. Keep the approach simple and direct.

Handwriting

Occasionally the employer asks for applications to be submitted in the candidate's own hand. This is usually because the employer believes — rightly or wrongly — that the neatness and style of an individual's writing gives some indication of his or her character.

Whilst you may think that this is all nonsense (and the worse your writing is, the more likely you are to say this), it is the employer who dictates the terms in these situations. If you ignore the instructions or dash off your usual scrawl, then you are unlikely to hear anything more.

If you should be asked to send handwritten applications and your presentation leaves a lot to be desired, then it would be worth a little effort to make some improvement. It is not suggested that you embrace the art of calligraphy, but rather that you start to take the trouble to make your writing as clear as possible. It may mean the difference between getting a job and missing one.

Staying efficient

Return all applications well before closing date. If no such date is given, then try to get the completed application in the employer's hands within a week, at the most, of the vacancy being announced.

In your diary make a note of the closing dates for applications and jot down reminders regarding enquiries which need to be made, follow-up letters to be sent, visits to be made, etc.

Keep a copy of the advertisement (or details obtained from other sources) for every job where you make an application, noting the publication and date it appeared. Any other information you have about the post or the employer should also be kept, together with copies of your written application, supporting letter and other related correspondence. Include the written note of the requirements for the job compared to your self-assessment, and your record of how the job measures up to your goals.

If the vacancy is filled and you are unsuccessful, add the evaluation you made of your performance. This material should then be taken out of the "live" file and stored elsewhere.

Before you complete an application for a job it is most important to ascertain the duties and responsibilities of the post, and also to get to know relevant details about the working environment.

Following earlier advice you will have evaluated the demands of the job and the qualities required from candidates — keep this assessment in the forefront of your mind when you are involved at all stages of the application. You will have a fair idea of what the employer is looking for — show him that he has found it!

11 COMPILING YOUR CURRICULUM VITAE

Preliminaries

Before you start to plan your C.V., try to consider who will be reading it and what their attitudes and expectations might be. Quite apart from the content of your application, its appearance, layout and style should be such that it will enhance your chances, rather than diminish them.

Remember that your adjudicators have foibles and prejudices, just like the rest of us. Since you cannot know what these are it is sensible to steer clear of any outrageously novel style of presentation.

Presentation

Use a good-quality A4 size white paper for your C.V. Sometimes candidates are advised to use a pale coloured paper since, it is argued, a C.V. written on, say, grey, light blue or ivory paper will be distinctive and give the person who uses it an edge over others. Remember, however, what has been stated about a novel approach and also consider that if the employer has your application photocopied to distribute to interested parties, then copies of your coloured paper will, in all probability, look far less presentable than the others.

Although you could write your C.V. if your handwriting is very good and you have a neat style, it is recommended that you have it typed or printed; the end result will be worth the trouble. Use just one side of the paper.

The length of your C.V. is important. Too short and the employer will have the immediate impression that you have little to offer; too long and he will have become bored before he has finished reading. Three pages is about right, although there will be some candidates who may feel they haven't enough material to fill three pages of A4 paper (e.g. school leavers, or women returning to work after a long spell at home with the children); people in this category should try to complete two pages.

Layout and language

Take care with the layout. It must be easy to read, with headings arranged in such an order that the reader will quickly form a clear picture of the candidate. Use underlining and sub-headings sparingly.

Employ good straightforward English; don't try to impress by using long words and keep technical expressions and abbreviations to a minimum.

The employer who insists on the use of an application form has determined what information the candidates must provide. A C.V., on the other hand, can be used by the applicant to present himself in the most favourable manner possible, although obvious gaps should be avoided.

It is strongly recommended that a different C.V. is presented for each application, except in the unlikely event of two identical posts being offered by different employers. By aiming your application at one specific post you are more likely to display your attributes in the best possible way.

It is essential that you send the original application, and not a copy.

The structure of your C.V.

On pages 59–64 are listed the headings you would use in compiling a Curriculum Vitae. It is not essential to use the term "Curriculum Vitae" if you prefer some other — e.g. "Personal History", "Personal Background and Experience", "Career History" or "Career Record".

Remember to aim your C.V. at one specific job — not only will the material come across as being fresh, but also you can be selective and slant the presentation when you have some awareness of what the employer is seeking.

Your letter and C.V. must be designed to make the reader feel that he / she must meet you and that you could well be the right person for the job.

C.V. HEADINGS

PERSONAL DETAILS

Name: Give full name

Address: Include post code, etc.

Telephone number: Include business phone number if practicable.

Date of birth: Not "age".

Marital status: State single or married; if married you could also mention number of children, if any. If divorced or separated then consider omitting this heading since some interviewers will react negatively.

Religion: Not always necessary — use your judgement.

Nationality: Not always necessary — use your judgement.

Current driving licence: Mention if appropriate.

EDUCATION

Schools: Names of schools with note of year commenced and year left. Involvement in school activities including sport. It is not necessary to give details of primary education.

College/University: Names and period attended. Extra-curricular activities and offices held. Any relevant achievements.

Further education: Name of institution and title of course, with relevant dates. (No mention of examinations passed under this heading.)

QUALIFICATIONS

                     List the examinations passed in chronological order. Use your discretion about mentioning the

QUALIFICATIONS (contd.)

grade of pass (if in the distant past it becomes less important; if the grades are not too good it might be wiser not to mention).
Membership of any professional association, offices held, etc.

TRAINING

Give details of all training received, whether formal (apprenticeships, articles, etc.), or informal, including any in-service training.
Mention new skills acquired or existing skills which have been improved. Proficiency in languages; with computer or word processor. An employer is likely to be favourably impressed by the fact that an applicant has not only qualifications and training which will be of direct benefit in the job on offer, but also has additional knowledge or skills. These may not be of immediate value but at least demonstrate that this person is versatile, industrious and probably has the capacity to improve.

EMPLOYMENT HISTORY

List your jobs in reverse order (i.e. the most recent job first), giving year commenced and year left. You would normally devote more space to the most recent employment than to jobs early in your career (unless, of course, there is something you wish to emphasise in an early post or you have a very short work record).
State the name of the employer

(together with a description of his field of work and location, if appropriate) and the description or title of your post. The responsibilities of each post should be clearly stated, with particular mention of employees under your supervision, tasks for which you were accountable; plant, machinery and buildings which were in your charge.

Take the opportunity to point out the skills which you were required to exercise in former posts, also any achievements where you could legitimately take the credit, either in your own particular sphere or for the wider benefit of your employer or your colleagues. Any training responsibilities, development of new methods, negotiation with Trade Unions. Any note of salary paid for previous employment loses much of its meaning because of the rapid rise in income in recent years and should be omitted, unless it would help your submission to give, say, your present salary (if the employer asks for details of previous salaries then, of course, this information must be supplied). Hopefully your employment record will show a steady progression from job to job; certainly promotions whilst with one employer should be recorded. There is normally little value in giving the reasons for leaving in your C.V. (you will probably be questioned on this subject at

EMPLOYMENT HISTORY (contd.)

interview), but this is a matter for each individual to decide.

Remember that it is the positive aspect of your career that you are advancing.

LEISURE INTERESTS

Although you may consider this subject rather irrelevant, it is sensible to include this heading in your C.V., since the interviewer will often be looking for an indication that there is some "depth" to the applicant, and that the candidate enjoys social and intellectual stimulation quite apart from his or her career interests.

Mention your hobbies and interests; any involvement in sport, community activities and membership of clubs, societies or national organisations. It is often wise not to include participation in certain spheres of activity which could antagonise the reader (e.g. membership of a political party). Interviewers frequently encourage applicants to talk about matters included in this section, since not only is it considered a sort of neutral area where the participants feel able to relax but also it might help to provide valuable insight into the character of the individual. The employer is interested in how you spend your spare time because it gives him a better understanding of you as an individual.

OBJECTIVES

The employer would usually welcome some indication from the applicant that his/her career objectives are appropriate and acceptable. Take great care here, however, since the impression can easily be given that you regard the job on offer merely as a means to an end, and that you would move on to something better as soon as practicable.

If you decide to include some contribution here, keep at the forefront of your mind the scope and prospects of the post which is offered and be prepared to argue that your previous experience is relevant and a good foundation for the developments you envisage. Make the objectives realistic, even if a little optimistic; there is nothing wrong with setting your sights high so long as your ambition remains within the bounds of possibility.

REFERENCES

The names, positions and addresses of two referees should be given (unless more are requested). Always remember to obtain their agreement before submitting their names.

Whilst it is commendable to have references from people in responsible positions who have some professional status, do remember that the most important requirement of a reference is that it should support the formal application and should also encourage the employer to believe that the person who is the subject of the enquiry has the personal qualities, experience and abilities to make a success of the position which is to be filled. An experienced interviewer can easily spot a reference which has obvious omissions or where a person's weaknesses or faults are being glossed over.

Choose your referees carefully, after having persuaded yourself that each one is likely to convince the reader of the strength of your application. An acceptable choice can often be your current employer (or employer from your recent past) as your first referee, with someone of status who can speak of your character as the second.

Employers don't necessarily abide by the unwritten rules, and it is not unknown for an employer to telephone referees and quiz them. You will have some idea what the referees have said about you; this may stimulate questions during the interview — so be prepared.

You may have in your possession a reference or testimonial from a former employer or someone of influence who writes glowingly of your qualities. By all means send along a copy (not the original) of this if you believe it will help, although the reader will realise that it was written in the knowledge that you would be reading it, and therefore its value might be questioned; also such a document may be out-of-date.

Style and presentation

In this section are set out two examples of C.V.s which will illustrate the points which have been made.

Note how the C.V.s are set out. Only one side of the paper should be used and headlines, underlining and capital letters are kept to a minimum. The effect is restrained, but business-like and pleasing. The facts are listed in a natural sequence, so that any area of interest can be quickly found.

Remember, however, that there may be circumstances (relating either to your personal history or to the situation on offer) which could indicate that it would be sensible to make some amendments to the recommended method of submission.

In these examples only rather limited details have been given. The interest of the reader should be stimulated and then he/she will, in all probability, wish to give that particular candidate the opportunity to elaborate on what has been written.

Candidates in other circumstances may wish to give more detail, and this is quite acceptable, but beware of too much embellishment. Arouse the employer's attention so that he/she will want to hear more (at interview).

C.V. Example 1 (see pp. 66–68)

A teenager about to finish full-time education is interested in employment as a Care Assistant in a home for the elderly. She hasn't got a brilliant record of scholastic achievement, but has lots of sound common sense and knows that this is the sort of work she would really enjoy.

Although she is rather young to be considered, she has some practical experience and awareness of the problems of dependent groups. She has worked in her spare time, and so she should not have much difficulty in adjusting to a working regime.

The fact that she has voluntarily become involved with the work of the Adult Training Centre shows some commitment to a career in a caring profession.

Her style of application (C.V. with accompanying short letter) will almost certainly compare very favourably with that of her competitors; applicants for jobs at this level very seldom present more than a handwritten one-page letter giving only an assortment of background details. She will undoubtedly be asked to attend for interview!

C.V. Example 2 (see pp. 68–72)

There is a vacancy for the post of Assistant Manager in a large hotel in the Midlands of the U.K. The candidate is relatively young and inexperienced, but has a record of both academic and professional achievement.

Example 1: **Curriculum Vitae**

PERSONAL

Name:	Eleanor TAVISTOCK
Address:	12 Durmiston Avenue, Arthurstown, Killinshire AW9 24RG
Telephone:	Arthurstown(1532) 2651
Date of Birth:	3rd. July, 1970
Marital Status:	Single

EDUCATION

School:	Arthurstown High School (1st team — Badminton)	1981–1986
College:	Killinshire Technical College (Member of Badminton Club)	1986 to date

QUALIFICATIONS

Scottish Vocational Educational Council	*Preliminary Certificate in Social Care*

QUALIFICATIONS (contd.)

	National Certificate (2-year course)	1987 to date
(Scotvec)	Passed in all ten modules of first year. Passed in first five modules of second year; currently completing remaining five modules. Practical experience — placements in School for Handicapped Children; Day Centre for Elderly and Home for Elderly.	

EMPLOYMENT

1987 to date	Part-time Assistant in Brown's Superstore (week-ends only).
1986 for 6 months	Delivery of morning papers.

LEISURE INTERESTS

Member of Arthurstown Badminton Club
For past three years I have helped the staff when there have been social functions at the local Adult Training Centre for the mentally handicapped.

OBJECTIVES

I would like to have a career where I could care for people who need help, and where there is the opportunity of promotion.

REFEREES

1	Mrs. E. Strickland. Principal, Killinshire Technical College, Broad Street, Arthurstown.
2	Mr. G. Nuttall. Officer in Charge, Arthurstown Adult Training Centre, Murdock Road, Arthurstown.

Example 2: **Curriculum Vitae**

PERSONAL

Name: Harold Richard ROBERTSON

Address: Flat 24,
South Granville Street,
Edinburgh
SD5 23BQ

Telephone: Home:
Edinburgh(031) 253127
Business: Edinburgh(031) 387619

Date of Birth: 18th October, 1965

Marital Status: Single

Religion: Church of Scotland

Nationality: British

EDUCATION

School: King's Academy, Near Dumfries
(1st. XI Football Team; member of Debating Society)   1979–1983

College: Kirkcudbright College of Technology
(Elected to Students' Representative Council)   1983–1986

QUALIFICATIONS

Scottish Certificate of Education Examination Board (S.C.E.E.B.)	*Ordinary Grade* English; Mathematics; Arithmetic; Chemistry; Biology; French	1981 'A' Pass
	Food & Nutrition; Art & Design	'B' Pass
S.C.E.E.B.	*Higher Grade* English; Art & Design Mathematics; Chemistry; Biology	1983 'B' Pass 'C' Pass
B.E.T.E.C.	Higher National Diploma in Hotel, Catering & Institutional Management	1986

TRAINING

Three-month part-time course "Cooking for the Catering Industry"
(Institute of Catering)
Good command of French language after spending many holidays in France.

1987

EMPLOYMENT HISTORY

1987 — present date *Assistant Food & Beverage Manager*
Grand Hotel, Princess Street, Edinburgh.
Required to provide liaison between Food and Beverage Manager and Hotel Administration.
Responsible for organisation and day-by-day running of popular restaurant within hotel (cover for 72

patrons).
In charge of Room Service facility.
Supervision of junior staff.
Whilst in post have organised a successful "Western Evening" with entertainment and appropriate menu for 150 people. Also a Burns' Supper for 80 guests.
During the past six months I have devised a "new look" menu in one of the restaurants and re-organised the food service to the guest rooms.
Awarded "Employee of the Month" in June and October, 1988.

1986–1987   *Trainee Assistant Manager*
Cross Guns Hotel, Dumfries.
Based in Reception area; in control of front office operations.
Supervision of Reception staff.
Responsibilities in connection with the organisation of restaurant and banqueting functions.
Latterly I was made accountable to the Manager for the arrangements and smooth running of all formal receptions and banquets.

1985 (7 weeks)   *Assistant Chef* — Dumfries

General Hospital
(practical placement from
College).
Basic food preparation in
all areas of kitchen.

1984 (11 weeks)   *General Assistant* — Cross
Guns Hotel, Dumfries
(practical placement from
College)
General work in all
Departments, including
kitchen, reception, bar and
dining room.
My office responsibilities
included organisation of
duty rota, routine clerical
tasks and filing.

LEISURE INTERESTS

I enjoy a game of golf and
have recently become
interested in weightlifting.
During the past two years I
have acquired a small
collection of "Art Deco"
pottery figures — I hope to
add to this in the future.

OBJECTIVES

My immediate plans are to
become involved in the
running of a highly rated
Country House hotel at
lower management level,
and eventually to become
a member of the top
management team.
I would hope to progress,
in time, to a senior
management post in a

OBJECTIVES (contd.)

hotel with an international
reputation, possibly
located in France.
Eventually I should like to
own and run a small hotel
which I could improve and
develop into an
establishment regarded as
one of the best of its kind.

REFEREES

1.

Mr. R. S. Regrout. General
Manager, Grand Hotel,
Princess Street, Edinburgh.
6BY 9KH.

2.

Mr. H. Davidson. Principal,
Kirkcudbright College of
Technology, Broad Street,
Kirkcudbright 2SH 7BF.

Interview expectations

A candidate's written application will usually stimulate questions
in the interview situation. It is sensible to re-read your copy of the
C.V. or application form before attending an interview so that
likely questions can be anticipated.

To illustrate this point it would not be too difficult to predict the
employer's probable lines of enquiry after receiving the Example 2
C.V.

Personal

*This is a senior post. Don't you think you are a little young to take
on so much responsibility?*
Response: The employer himself cannot really believe this or he
would not have invited you for interview. Remind him of the
advantages of youth, the responsible tasks you have already
undertaken, and the width of your experience in your short working life.

You have lived and worked in Scotland all your life; would you not find it a big wrench to move three hundred miles to the Midlands?
Response: Stress your adaptability and your belief that it is not so much where you are, as what you are doing and who your colleagues are that is important.

Education and Qualifications

You have done quite well in examinations; did you ever think of pursuing an academic career?
Response: Emphasise your belief that it is important to work in a field where you have talent and a keen interest.

Training

Why take a cooking course when your present job and future plans are in hotel management?
Response: To be a really effective manager one has to understand the organisation and problems of all aspects of the establishment. The reputation of a hotel can stand or fall by the standard of the meals it provides and the catering course helped to provide more insight of the work performed by kitchen staff.

Employment history

Since leaving college you have had two jobs, working in each for about a year. Would you not agree that it is wiser to stay longer in a position so that you have the full benefit of all the experience available?
Response: You could state that in both your jobs you have been fortunate in having been given a wide and stimulating range of responsibilities. You might mention that you appreciate you still have much to learn in your present post, but the advertised position offers such exciting possibilities that you felt you could not let this opportunity go by (you will then be asked what you mean by "exciting possibilities" — be prepared for obvious supplementary questions).

Leisure interests

Why did you give up football?
Response: The hours I work mean that I cannot undertake commitments on a regular basis in my spare time. The arrangements for playing golf can be more flexible.

Tell us about "Art Deco".
Response: Make sure you know enough about your stated interest to be able talk about it interestingly for a couple of minutes.

Objectives

It is certain that you will be closely questioned about your stated goals.
Response: Ensure that you have thought out how you will elaborate on your written statement; particularly how you will counter any suggestion that you would not stay long in this job, if it were offered.

In your written submission, and later in your discussion when interviewed, it is most important that you are positive in your approach. Show that you are eager for new challenges and optimistic about the future.

12   PREPARING FOR THE INTERVIEW

If, after making an application for a job you receive an invitation to attend for interview, then you deserve to congratulate yourself — you have successfully negotiated the first major hurdle.

Most of your competitors will have been eliminated. Since the employer naturally does not want to spend valuable time talking to people he would not employ, it follows that any one of the persons who is short-listed can be offered the appointment.

Adequate preparation should ensure that you have an excellent chance of being the chosen candidate.

Remember to confirm that you will attend.

Preliminaries

There are certain obvious preparations which have to be made before attending for interview — but the fact that many of these are clearly evident does not mean that they should not be stated. It is amazing how many people jeopardise their chances by being slipshod about elementary arrangements.

Be clear as to where and when the interview is being held. Make sure that you allow sufficient time for travelling, parking, etc., so that you arrive before the appointed time.

You will, of course, be smartly dressed for your interview. Unless you have very good reason to believe that an unusual style would be favourably received, it is wise to be conventional in appearance. You may say that you will dress as you please and no-one is going to decide how you should look! If you really want the job you are seeking then it is as well to remember that no interviewer can be entirely objective, and no matter how professionally organised the interview may be, the participants' personal feelings, doubts and prejudices will influence their judgement; an unacceptable appearance may just tip the scales against you.

Read carefully all the correspondence which may have arrived with your letter inviting you for interview. If you believe that you should know more about the job or the employer's business then do more research, enlisting as much help as you can from both official and other sources. The more knowledgeable you show yourself to be, the more likely you are to impress at interview.

Job appraisal

You will have formed some idea of what personal qualities, qualifications and experience the employer is looking for in the ideal candidate when evaluating the job (Chapter 9). Have another look at what you believe you can offer (Chapter 4 on Personal Qualities). Remind yourself of your own strengths and consider how best you can bring these to the attention of the interviewer without appearing immodest.

Motivation and attitudes

Before the day of the interview sort out your feelings about the post which is being offered. Discuss it with close members of your family or trusted friends and find out their views about the alteration in your circumstances if you were to be successful.

It is not unknown for a candidate to accept the offer of a job, then shortly afterwards to advise the employer that he cannot take up the post (because, for example, his wife doesn't want to move!). In these circumstances the employer is understandably rather annoyed, and may well feel disposed to pass the word around — the candidate could then find it very difficult to obtain another appointment in his field.

Curiously one often meets other candidates in an interview situation who tell you that they don't really want the job! If they are being truthful then they should have stayed at home.

In everything you undertake relating to job-searching, you must be positive in your approach. If you are half-hearted in your efforts then the results are likely to be poor; the nearer you get to the interview then the more determined you must be — this is the attitude that wins jobs. Determination is the characteristic which distinguishes people at the top of commerce, government and the professions from others who never seem to make much headway.

Purposeful preparation

Occasionally in an interview you may be asked to discuss some current event. Since, with most jobs, your awareness of current affairs is of no relevance to the work you will be required to undertake, you may think this is hardly "playing the game". Nevertheless the rules of the interview are drawn up by the employer and you just have to go along with them. If you are unable to give an adequate account of yourself in such a conversation then it will not help your presentation.

If you are not in the habit of keeping abreast of the news then perhaps you should alter your habits, at least until you have successfully landed a job; try reading one of the "quality" Sunday newspapers every week.

Likely questions

You may be asked to elaborate on any aspect of your application, or on any discrepancies, omissions and irrelevancies in your written submission. As stated earlier, you must make sure that you read over, with care, the copy you have kept and note any obvious area of enquiry, so that you are prepared.

It is possible to anticipate some of the questions that you are likely to have to answer at most interviews. Whilst it would be unwise to rehearse a series of carefully thought-out answers to typical questions, it is certainly helpful conscientiously to consider how you would answer searching enquiries on topics which are likely to be raised.

The interviewer will ask different questions for different purposes. The first few minutes of an interview are usually spent in trying to put the candidate at ease and in establishing a relationship between the interviewer and the applicant; unloaded questions like "Did you have a good journey?" can be expected at this stage.

Subsequent questioning will be aimed at discovering what sort of person you are, what your motivation is, whether or not your qualifications and experience really do equip you for the job, how you are likely to get along with future colleagues and if you are capable of exercising (and taking) supervision.

There are some customary questions you can anticipate (in addition to those aroused by your written application), and it is useful to be aware of the most popular of these.

Here is a selection of questions which cover the main areas of interest to employers. Not all the questions listed will be asked at every interview, of course, but you should spend some time in thinking how you would answer each one in such a manner that your replies will improve your case. Adequate preparation in this area is very important.

1. *Why do you want the job? or What is there about this post that attracts you?*

2. *Why did you leave your last job(s)?*

3. *What do you find unsatisfactory in your present job?*

4. *What qualities have you which fit you for the post?*

5. *What would you be looking for in a candidate if you were in my shoes?*

6. *I have seen what you have written, now tell me about yourself.*

7. *Explain to me what you do in your present (previous) post(s).*

8. *Do you consider your qualifications adequate for the work you are seeking?*

9. *Tell me about some of your achievements at work.*

10. *How relevant is your experience?*

11. *What has given you the most satisfaction in your previous employment?*
    What has caused you the most difficulty?

12. *Are there some people you find it difficult to work with?*

13. *How healthy are you?*

14. *What are you strengths and weaknesses?*

15. *Who is your favourite author?*

16. *Convince me that you can cope with responsibility.*

17. *How would you change things if you got the job? or What is the first thing you would do if you got the job?*

18. *What is your ambition?*

19. *If appointed, how long would you stay with us?*

20. *If you are offered the job, when can you start?*

21. *What salary are you looking for?*

22. *Do you know anyone who works here?*

23. Is there anything you would like to ask me?

If you have put into practice the advice in previous chapters you will now discover, when considering the above questions, how helpful that preparation proves to be. It is not proposed to go through each of the above questions, but hints about answering selected ones will be useful.

2 and 3: Take care not to be too critical of your past and present employers.

14: Don't say that you have no weaknesses (this might be taken to indicate arrogance or lack of insight), but rather admit to "weaknesses" which have positive aspects (e.g. "I can too easily see the other person's point of view", or "I have such high standards for myself that I can seldom achieve them").

17: Although you may feel that there are some areas within the responsibilities of the post where you would like to make changes, it may be unwise to say so at this stage. Rather state that you would need some time in the post before recommending changes — if you have a clear idea where you could improve things you might hint that you would pay particular attention to these items as soon as possible.

21: If the salary is not fixed then it is as well to decide before the interview what salary you would seek (make enquiries about the going rate for similar jobs). You could be a little ambitious in your request, without being unreasonable, but be prepared to justify your figure.

22: If you know someone working for the same employer, then it will be expected that you have talked to that person.

23: Any further questions? Applicants are usually given the opportunity to ask questions. Even when the interviewer doesn't give you the opening it is quite acceptable, at the end of the interview, to say "May I ask for clarification of one or two points?", or words to that effect.

If all the information you need has been given in the hand-outs and during the interview then, of course, it is unnecessary for you to ask further questions. Remember, however, that employers will often consider questions from the candidate to be evidence that he/she is thinking carefully about the post on offer and this should weigh in that person's favour.

There would not usually be any objection to you producing a prepared list of points you had decided to raise. When asking questions remember to be positive (e.g. training and promotion prospects, opportunities to develop the job, how your work will be assessed); questions about salary, pension scheme, holidays and so on are legitimate, but too many such questions will cause the employer to doubt your motives. Avoid queries about trivial matters.

Some interviewers are fond of asking hypothetical questions. This is a hazardous area and such enquiries are best dealt with by relating your answer to something similar in your own experience — you can then speak with knowledge and confidence.

Occasionally there may be a deliberate ploy to pass the initiative to you. If there is a specific theme then you can deal with it, but if it is very open-ended you may be caught out unless you are prepared. Decide which subject you would wish to expand on if presented with this dilemma, and note the points you would make.

Practice

Almost everyone will benefit from some practice (out loud) in answering expected questions; you could use a tape recorder for this purpose and listen to yourself improve with practice. If you can persuade a trusted and skilful friend to put you through a mock interview then so much the better, although an acquaintance who might be a rival would not be a wise choice.

Re-read the copy of your Application the day before your interview.

If you take the trouble to make yourself ready for your interview in the manner which has been suggested then you will have the satisfaction of knowing that your preparation has almost certainly been more thorough than any of your competitors.

A word of warning

It is possible to do too much and to be over-prepared; judge when to finish so that you are as relaxed as possible for your interview. Tell yourself that you will try to enjoy the challenge which it represents. If you go into the room with this feeling then you may be agreeably surprised by what you achieve!

13 THE INTERVIEW

Arriving for interview

Remember what has been said about style of dress and the importance of ensuring that you arrive in good time (i.e. about ten minutes before the appointment). On no account should you take tranquillisers or alcohol to get you through the encounter.

It is not only in the interview room where judgements are made; from the moment you meet the receptionist (who sometimes has influence far exceeding her status) to the time when you walk out of sight of the building you are being assessed.

Take with you the following items (ideally in a document case):

1) Copy of the completed application form or C.V., together with letter inviting you for interview and any related correspondence.

2) The originals of any testimonials you have given.

3) Evidence of qualifications (certificates, etc.).

4) List of questions you have prepared.

5) Daily paper or book to help pass the time whilst waiting.

The waiting room

In the waiting room you may, or may not, be introduced to your competitors. Try to relax and don't be too impressed by the apparent confidence that the others show; you probably seem just as confident to them. Occasionally there are one or two candidates who use the waiting time to try and impress the opposition, presumably in the hope that this will demoralise everyone. Try to ignore this sort of performance — it is the interviewer who requires to be impressed, not you.

Almost everyone finds the period spent waiting to be summoned for interview a nerve-racking one. If there are others waiting then you could find it helpful to have a friendly conversation with them. If you are alone then keep busy; look at any magazines in the room or read the daily paper or book you have brought.

A heightened anxiety is not necessarily a bad thing — with the adrenalin flowing you can be on top form!

Purpose of interview

The interview is usually the principal means by which an employer decides which candidate is suitable for a job on offer.

It can be argued that a person's performance at interview can only test how that individual copes with interviews, and will not necessarily indicate how good he or she will be in the job. Nevertheless, this is by far the most common method used by employers and since you cannot alter the rules, it is sensible to accept the situation and make sure that your interview technique and performance is as good as you can make it.

Most interviewers try to create an atmosphere which will help candidates to relax and make the most of their opportunity (also the interviewer finds it easier to make evaluations when defences are lowered).

Generally speaking, employers want to employ people who are competent, reliable, mature, enthusiastic and have some ambition. Their objective is to fill all vacancies with employees who will prove to be an asset in their organisation.

Interview framework

An interview can be structured and rigid, or informal and flexible — most fall somewhere between the extremes.

The interview will usually take place in the interviewer's own office, or in a room which is used for meetings and similar purposes. Candidates may all be called to attend at the same time, or the appointments will be arranged so that there is as little waiting time as possible. It is common practice for applicants to be seen in alphabetical order.

The interviewer will welcome you and, if there are other people present, will usually introduce them to you. Try to remember the interviewer's name (and others if you can). You may be expected to shake hands, but wait for this to be made clear before you do so. You will be invited to sit down, and there will usually follow one or two observations or questions designed to put you at your ease, e.g. about the weather, or your journey.

The interview proper will often commence with the interviewer describing the job on offer (and possibly stating what sort of person they are looking for). There may also be some statement made about the employer's business and philosophy.

The next stage will most likely be a discussion centred around your written application. You will be given the opportunity to expand on what you have written (your employment history will attract particular scrutiny), to explain any gaps or apparent discrepancies in your records and generally to sell yourself as an individual with the skills, imagination and motivation to make a success of the job which is being offered.

At the end of the interview you may be offered the post or told that you have been unsuccessful; on the other hand you may be advised that you will be informed of the decision in due course.

The employer's representative will usually make notes on each candidate's performance, personality, background and potential — and the appointment will be made on the basis of this assessment.

Interviewers will often have a structured basis to their questions; the more skilled the interviewer, the less easy this is to detect. He or she will wish to cover the following points:

Status:	Health; appearance; speech; home circumstances.
Qualifications:	Sound educational basis. Qualifications relevent and up to date.
Experience:	Does the employment record justify confidence?
Interests:	Abilities and aptitudes; leisure pursuits.
Personality:	Warmth; ability to develop relationships (and lead others).
Intellect:	Able to cope with demands of job; imaginative.
Suitability:	Attitudes; drive; enthusiasm.

The interviewer

Whatever the setting or the style of the interview, it is the personality, manner and competence of the interviewer which will determine, to a large extent, whether or not you feel at ease in this rather artificial situation.

He/she may be professionally involved with the appointment of all staff for the employer, possibly in the Personnel Department. In that case you would reasonably expect expertise and professionalism to be demonstrated in the conduct of the interview. It must be said, though, that not all the people professionally engaged in the appointment of staff show skill in managing an interview.

An Agency interviewer is likely to show the most skill, and to be less easily influenced by personal factors. He/she will have a clear understanding of the duties of the post and of the employer's expectations. Care will be taken to make each candidate aware of all the important conditions of service and to cover all the essential points listed above. This interviewer is likely to be more objective in his/her judgement than most, and therefore a candidate who is well prepared has no particular reason to be anxious.

More often than not you will discover that the interviewer is someone who has this responsibility because he/she has a certain position and status with the employer, perhaps the person in charge of the section where the new employee will work; in a small firm it may be the employer himself. Unfortunately the proficiency of a person in his work and his standing with the firm do not guarantee any degree of competence as an interviewer.

Remember, therefore, that the person who interviews you may not have much belief in his/her own ability in this situation and may be just as nervous as you are. If you can sense that this is the case then you could, if you have enough self-confidence, take some initiative yourself — do take care, however, not to let it appear as if you are taking over the interview.

No matter how fair and unbiased the employer's representative tries to be, it is very difficult for most people to be objective when making choices between individuals. We all have our likes and dislikes (others call them prejudices). With insight some people can deal with this, but judgements can be influenced by personal feelings and experiences. Since you can do nothing about this it is as well to ignore it and get on with making the most of your opportunity.

First impressions

The interviewer, or interviewing panel, will take the initiative when you enter the room, but your appearance and conduct in those first few minutes are crucial, and set the scene for the remainder of your discussion. There may be a feeling of friendliness and informality encouraged, but remember that you are being weighed up from the first moment of your meeting.

Take pains to be pleasant and cheerful in your approach; when spoken to look that person in the eye as you reply. Shake hands if you can see that this is expected of you and sit down if invited to do so (but not on the edge of your chair). Address the person who speaks to you by name from time to time. Respond clearly when spoken to. Although it will help your image if you appear to be at ease, it would be most unwise to carry this to the lengths of, say, taking off your jacket or lighting a cigarette.

Rapport

The effectiveness of an interview depends very largely upon the relationship which develops between the interviewer(s) and the candidate. The interviewer's manner can determine not only the style of the discussion but also whether or not the participants feel at ease and therefore likely to perform well.

The candidate must go half-way in creating a helpful atmosphere. It is important that the interviewer and interviewee get along together: only in these circumstances will a positive relationship develop where the employer's representative shows a genuine interest in what the applicant has to say and where the person being interviewed feels able to relax and give of his/her best. The interview will then become a discussion rather than an interrogation.

Occasionally you may meet an interviewer who is rude, either by natural temperament or in a deliberate attempt to create tension. The theory behind this style is apparently that any candidate who can cope adequately with antagonism when being considered for appointment can cope equally well with stress at work. It has never been shown that there is any basis to this supposition. All that a stressful interview will really achieve is to test that candidate's ability to cope with a stressful interview!

If you encounter rudeness on the part of the interviewer then you must keep calm; don't be tempted into retaliating in a similar vein. Do not suffer humiliation but rather demonstrate that you can rise above it. Of course you would consider whether or not you want to work for someone who behaves like this, but that person may not be at all representative of other senior staff.

Sometimes silence is used as a method of interview (everyone who works in the field of human relationships is aware of how effective a tool silence can be). Keep cool — if nothing is said after some little time say something like "Would you like me to elaborate on anything we have discussed?" The initiative is then handed back to the interviewer.

Even in the most encouraging interview where there is a feeling of equality, informality and friendliness, remember that the interviewer is in control and is quietly assessing your potential.

The employer's representative will give candidates the chance to show that they can develop and use relationships; he will want to be convinced that they can work in harmony with others. He is probably a busy person with a multitude of problems waiting for him when he returns to his normal duties. He is looking for someone who, having the necessary qualifications, experience, aptitudes and motivation will get along with his/her new colleagues. The last thing he wants is to discover that this new appointee is going to add to his worries.

Tactics

Preliminaries If you have carried out your preliminary enquiries thoroughly, as advised, you will know the purpose of the job, its main responsibilities and its role in the organisation. You should also have a good idea what background, experience and personal qualities the employer is likely to be looking for. Keep this image in your mind throughout the interview.

Since you have taken the trouble painstakingly to prepare yourself for this moment and have also sent in a first class application, you must know that you have the advantage of your less thorough competitors (and very few, if any, will be so well prepared). Take comfort from this.

It is not unusual to find that you are very anxious at this stage (perhaps perspiring, with a dry mouth and a sinking feeling in your stomach). Try deep breathing immediately before you go into the interview room, this usually helps. With some people a little anxiety has the effect of increasing perception and alertness, so this can be a positive factor.

Sit down when invited, try to relax and not to fidget. Look alert but relaxed and confident (even if you don't feel it) — remember that your "body language" can be revealing, so show the interviewer by your behaviour and attitude that you are in control of yourself and eager to make the most of this opportunity. How you behave can be almost as revealing as what you say!

Communication Use plain English without frills or jargon, and speak in your normal style. An open and candid manner will impress, as will the correct approach to the interviewer — a hint of deference is acceptable, but not an ingratiating approach. Address the interviewer by name — "Sir" or "Ma'm" is unnecessary (except in the Armed Forces).

Often people who are nervous speak too quickly. If this describes you then you must make the conscious effort to slow down.

Show that you believe in yourself. If you dither and show uncertainty how can you expect the employer to believe in you?

Throughout the discussion remember to be positive; show your determination and enthusiasm. Speak clearly, wait until the interviewer has finished speaking before you answer, and make sure that your answers are more than "yes" or "no", without being too garrulous.

Try to allow a little of your personality to peep through when answering questions; if you have the opportunity then don't be afraid to demonstrate that you have a sense of humour. If the interviewer likes you then your chances of appointment will increase enormously!

Substance Most candidates believe that the interviewer will want to talk about details of their background. Some time will certainly be spent in discussing each applicant's knowledge and attainments, but in reality interviewers are more interested in looking beyond the catalogue of qualifications, experience, etc., and discovering what sort of person the applicant is, how he or she behaves, what the real motivation is for the application and how he or she would fit in if offered the post.

Age If it is hinted that you are too young or too old for the job remind yourself that the employer knew your age before he invited you for interview, and presumably he would not wish to waste his time seeing people whom he had no intention of appointing. If you are young, tell him that you have the attributes of youth, e.g. energy, flexibility of outlook, enthusiasm, ability to learn quickly and few family ties. If you are older, then point out that age can be a positive attribute, since it offers a width of experience, dependability and maturity of approach which is hard to find in a younger person.

Diplomacy   Steer clear of topics which invite argument, e.g. politics and religion, unless, of course, the post is in a related field of employment.

If you are a woman with a family then you are likely to be asked about your caring arrangements if the children are sick or on holiday (see Chapter 7). What the employer wants to know, of course, is whether or not your commitments at home would interfere with your obligations at work.

You must always be truthful in your replies. It is expected, however, that you would make the most of your strongest attributes and avoid, if possible, long discussion in areas where it would be wise to say as little as possible. An example to illustrate this point is of an applicant, when asked if he is in good health, replying "Yes; I had a serious illness three years ago but I made a complete recovery." The employer thought he had better check on this person's health before offering the job and, with his permission, wrote to his doctor. The doctor's reply was ambiguous and the employer decided to appoint someone else rather than take a chance! This applicant could have answered (truthfully) "Yes, I am in good health".

Searching questions about your present or previous employers might require to be answered with some diplomacy. Do not criticise past employers since the person who is listening to this criticism may feel that if this candidate were appointed, it may then become his turn to be criticised. Also, criticism of one's boss is sometimes used as an excuse for one's own failings. Any attempt to elicit restricted information about your present job would also require to be parried.

When you cannot easily understand a question, then ask for clarification. This is much better than floundering.

Negotiations about salary is expected in some situations; this should be undertaken with delicacy, not in the form of an ultimatum.

Don't forget to take the opportunity to ask questions, either those which you have prepared beforehand or others which may have been raised in your mind during the course of the conversation.

Ending   At the end of the interview you may be offered the job, advised that you have been unsuccessful or told that you will be contacted later with the result. If you are offered the job and there are elements of the offer which require thought, then ask for a little time for consideration.

Leave the room with dignity, thanking the interviewer for his/her interest.

Interviews with different structures

Panel interview   Where a group of people, with a chairman, interviews all the applicants. This is a popular method with public appointments, when most of the participants could be elected members with little or no specialised knowledge. A copy of your application will almost certainly have been circulated to all members of the panel. Each person will probably have decided what he/she wants to talk to you about, and so you are likely to have to respond to a wide range of questions but may not have the time or opportunity to develop your themes as you would wish.

Since the opportunity to sell yourself will be more fleeting in this situation, with most panel members wahting to demonstrate that they have a useful contribution to make, it is important to make the most of the openings you are given. Study the copy of your C.V. or application form and decide which areas you will be required to amplify; now consider carefully how you can develop your answers so that you highlight those qualities, skills or experiences which will enhance your submission.

Although the chairman controls the meeting and ostensibly is the most important person present, in practice there may well be someone at the meeting whose influential opinion will govern the decision. This person can often be identified since he/she will be shown special regard by the chairman, and questions from this quarter will be particularly searching.

Ensure that you look directly at the questioner when answering, even though you may be aware that more prestigious members are listening.

Sequential interviews   There are several variations of this style, usually reserved for the more important jobs. There could be, for instance, an initial informal meeting with future colleagues, followed by a shorter meeting with a senior person and ending with a formal interview session by a panel.

It isn't possible to sustain any artificial attitudes or pretences throughout all these discussions (indeed, it is never advisable to try to hoodwink your interviewers). Be yourself; decide the purpose of each session and keep this in mind. Remember that you want this job and that you believe you can do it well.

If you have been short-listed with others who have to go through this ordeal, then you may be sure that you are a serious contender. The employer is not going to waste the time of all these people in seeing someone who hasn't a chance; quite apart from any other consideration his judgement would appear to be suspect, and this he would not like.

Group methods These can take several forms, and are usually designed so that candidates are placed in a situation where their conduct, skills and ability to form meaningful relationships can be noted, to be borne in mind when the formal interview takes place.

As an example, all the applicants are asked to discuss together a contrived situation relating to their expertise, and to devise an appropriate course of action. The group will then probably organise itself for its task, with a chairman and secretary, and observers will see how relationships are formed, how individuals exercise authority, who is clear thinking and articulate and who is inclined to be diverted into matters of inconsequence; how the group copes with leadership issues and who stays silent and takes a back seat.

If you are required to participate in any such exercise, remember that it will not help your standing if you don't take an active part — shyness must be overcome. If you are given the chance to assume any responsibility then accept it; show leadership qualities if you can, but not at others' expense. Demonstrate that you can handle a situation and that you can play a significant role in helping to reach the goal. Take care not to be patronising, condescending or rude; this would show a lack of consideration for others and would not help your image.

You will require to demonstrate that you are able to make a full contribution to the group effort. Although you wish to do well, you should also take care to involve others in the group (a successful executive uses all the talent available to him). Show that you are a calm, cheerful, competent person with a sense of humour.

Tests On occasions an interview will incorporate an I.Q. test or a psychological test designed to highlight aptitudes, confidence, extrovert or introvert tendencies, sociability, assertiveness, etc.

There is very little evidence to support the argument that tests such as these will help to show who is the best person for a particular post. Indeed, one school of thought maintains that the true purpose is to relieve the decision-maker of the responsibility for bad appointments.

If you have to take such a test remember the assessment you have made of the qualities which are being sought; it is surprising how helpful this can be when answering questions!

The above styles of interview are not exhaustive, but are the ones commonly met. Whatever you are required to face, whether it is a short informal chat with an agreeable representative or a long exhausting series of meetings, remember that the principles set out in this book apply to all such situations. The employer wants to meet a candidate he likes, who appears to have the right background, temperament and ability to do the job well and to advance the interests of the employer.

However skilled you are you will not be offered all the jobs you apply for. Consider that you are no worse off than before if you fail an interview — in fact you are better off since you have had this experience and will, no doubt, have learned from it!

14 AFTER THE INTERVIEW

How well did you cope?

It is quite common to leave an interview feeling that you could have done better, or remembering something that you should have said. Most of the candidates will feel the same (although they are unlikely to admit it).

As soon as possible after the interview you should consider making an assessment of your performance. This is a chore that you might feel unwilling to take on, particularly if you believe that you could have done better, but it can pay dividends in the future.

Look at your self-assessment records and note those qualities which you rated highly. Did you manage to get these across in the interview? If not, why not? Were you calm, confident and positive in your manner?

If there were any unexpected questions then they are likely to be asked again. Make a note and consider your answer when next asked.

Each interview gives you valuable practice in improving your presentation, so even if you are not to be offered the job your next interview should be that much easier and more productive. As with other things, you will improve with practice.

Keep all your notes and correspondence relating to each job you apply for and file it away. Anything you have learned you can add to your ongoing notes for future use.

Follow-up letter

Unless you have been advised that there will be a formal notification within a specified time it is recommended that you send a letter, addressed to the person who interviewed you, within a few days.

This letter should reaffirm your interest in the job, mention matters raised by the interviewer (either about the post or the firm) which you could say interested (intrigued, impressed) you. You could also say that you enjoyed the interview, which confirmed your view that your experience and abilities would be an asset to the firm. End the letter by stating that you hope you will have the opportunity of working with the firm and look forward to hearing the decision.

This reminder, in which you are still selling yourself (this time a "soft" sell), will ensure that you at least, out of all the candidates, will be remembered.

Study the example of a follow-up letter given here.

Follow-up Letter

22 Cromley Court,
Brunton,
Mr. R. W. Smithson,   Mirtleshire
Assistant Director of Social
  Services
Social Services Department,   Tel: Brunton 2537
County Hall,
Brunton.
BR2 KL6   12th February, 1989

Dear Mr. Smithson,

Team Leader

I am writing to record my appreciation of the stimulating discussion we had yesterday when I attended interview for the above post.

The possibility of working for a Social Services Authority which encourages all grades of staff to advance their own ideas for discussion (and perhaps implementation) by senior management is one which I find exciting. I am sure that this policy helps to attract many first-class workers to the Department and I believe that my experience with the launching of a similar scheme together with my involvement in specialist roles would be of unique and practical value in this position.

I would like to confirm my keen interest in the appointment and look forward to hearing from you in the near future.

Yours sincerely,

(Arthur H. Waddington)

Offer of appointment

If you are advised that you have been successful, then you should receive confirmation in writing. Ensure that you do, and send a letter confirming your acceptance within 24 hours (unless you have changed your mind or wish to query something in the conditions).

Wait until you have the offer in writing before giving in your notice in your current job.

Rejection

How easy it is to feel dejected when you learn that you haven't got the job you had set your heart on. Nevertheless, you must persevere in your efforts.

Regard each interview as a separate experience from which you can learn. It is important to ensure that you are continually planning future applications — all your eggs were not in that one basket!

Examine carefully your written and oral performance as advised above. If you cannot identify where you fell short of your best then it might be useful to discuss the matter frankly and in detail with a friend. Be cautious, however, since the person you confide in must not only be capable, knowledgeable and objective; he must also be worthy of trust.

There are many more candidates than there are jobs available. Even very good candidates are not guaranteed success every time, and there are sometimes factors (e.g. personal foibles of the employer) which could not have been foreseen.

It is vitally important that you do not lose heart with one or two failures. Keep plugging away; use the methods described in this book and be realistic in your search. Your aim is to achieve something that can change the course of your whole future; it is worth a lot of effort.

FINAL WORDS

Having read this book you now have at your fingertips clear and detailed advice on every important aspect of job-seeking.

The knowledge, guidance, hints and encouragement which are contained in these pages will be invaluable to you in your future endeavours, but the effort must come from you and must be sustained.

It is helpful to remind yourself that almost all the people who have achieved real success in their chosen field of work have done so not because they were brilliant or had marvellous strokes of good luck, but rather because they have shown dogged determination in achieving their goal, and have the capability for sustained hard work.

It is important to establish and maintain a routine in job-hunting; a systematic, constructive approach will pay the best dividends. Keep abreast of the vacancies on offer, ensure records are kept up to date, check the closing date for applications and make sure that everything is posted in good time.

One important fact which is seldom acknowledged is that it is not necessarily the best applicant who is offered the job. The fortunate candidate is the person who has submitted a good enough application to merit an interview and then impressed enough at interview to outshine the competition!

If you are equal to the job you have chosen and have followed the guidelines set out in this book, then you have an excellent chance of being the person who is selected.

GOOD LUCK!